CRAVE
TORONTO

The Urban Girl's Manifesto

Melody Biringer

CRAVE Toronto: The Urban Girl's Manifesto

A publication of The CRAVE Company
1805 12th Ave W #A
Seattle WA 98119
206.282.0173

thecravecompany.com/toronto
twitter.com/cravetoronto
facebook.com/cravetoronto

While every effort was made to ensure the accuracy of the information, details are subject to change so please call ahead. Neither The CRAVE Company nor CRAVE Toronto shall be responsible for any consequences arising from the publication or use.

All editorial content in this publication is the sole opinion of CRAVE Toronto and our contributing writers. No fees or services were rendered in exchange for inclusion in this publication.

Printed in the United States of America

ISBN 978-0-9847143-6-0
Second Edition
August 2012
$19.95 CAD

The Urban Girl's Manifesto

We CRAVE Community.
We believe in acknowledging, celebrating and passionately supporting local businesses. CRAVE is a celebration of women entrepreneurs that showcases creative, interesting and gutsy proprietors. By introducing you to the savvy businesswomen in this guide, we hope that we will help inspire your own inner entrepreneur.

We CRAVE Adventure.
We encourage you to break your routine, to venture away from your regular haunts, to visit new businesses, to explore all the funky finds and surprising spots that Toronto has to offer. Whether it's to hunt for a birthday gift, indulge in a spa treatment or connect with like-minded people, let CRAVE Toronto be your guide for a one-of-a-kind hometown adventure.

We CRAVE Quality.
CRAVE is all about quality products and thoughtful service. We know that a satisfying shopping trip requires more than a simple exchange of money for goods, and that a rejuvenating spa date entails more than a quick clip of the cuticles and a swipe of polish. We know you want to come away feeling uplifted, beautiful, excited, relaxed, relieved and, above all, knowing you got the most bang for your buck. We have scoured the city to find the hidden gems, new hot spots and old standbys, all with one thing in common: they're the best of the best!

Introduction

A Guide to Our Guide

CRAVE Toronto is more than a guidebook. It's a savvy, quality-of-lifestyle book devoted entirely to local businesses owned by women. CRAVE Toronto will direct you to some of the best local spots—top boutiques, spas, cafés, stylists, fitness studios and more. And we'll introduce you to the inspired, dedicated women behind these exceptional enterprises, for whom creativity, quality, innovation and customer service are paramount.

Not only is CRAVE Toronto an intelligent guide for those wanting to know what's happening throughout town, it's a directory for those who value the contributions that spirited businesswomen make to our region.

Myrlene Sundberg

Q&A

What are your most popular products or services?
Our speciality is well-designed furnishings for small spaces. Furniture that is multifunctional.

What tip would you give women who are starting a business?
Don't be afraid to fail. You learn from your failures.

What motivates you on a daily basis?
Accomplishments. I am self-motivated, and accomplishments are what motivate me.

What place inspires you and why?
I love travelling, and I especially love London, Paris and Milan. I find the architecture inspiring.

Photos by Lemon Fresh Designs Photography

Urban Mode

145 Tecumseth St, Toronto, 416.591.8834, info@urbanmode.com
urbanmode.com, facebook.com/urbanmodedesign, Twitter: @theurbanmode

Innovative. Vibrant. Inspiring.
Urban Mode showcases modern furniture and accessories, with a flair for
colour and design. One of the first lifestyle stores in Canada, Urban Mode
is celebrating its 35th year in business. Myrlene and her experienced
design team are always available for sourcing, space planning and offering
design solutions. Their motto is: Smart Design for Small Spaces.

" I love the independence of owning a business. I love being able to create it however I want it. "

Myrlene Sundberg of Urban Mode

ᴵ Q&A

What are your most popular products or services?
Our readers are most happy with the personal approach we take toward our interviews. We don't just want to know about your art, we want to learn about you.

What tip would you give women who are starting a business?
Get out there! Go to events, not just for networking but for the experience. Immerse yourself in your business and really get to know and understand those you're helping.

What do you like best about owning a business?
The interviews. To see the artist behind the work, the owner behind the development or the inventor of a product allows you to enter their personal story and publish it.

What motivates you on a daily basis?
The idea of learning and evolving makes me excited to do what I do. Getting that special interview or discovering a new place makes it all worth the work.

What is your motto or theme song?
My theme song is definitely "Vienna" by Billy Joel. I've always been an overachiever, but sometimes you have to learn to step back and listen to your needs.

Jessica Di Loreto

Acid City
Online Magazine

416.400.1250, acidcitymag.com, Twitter: @AcidCityMag

Opinionated. Bold. Beautiful.
Acid City is the new trendsetter's guide on pop culture in today's society. It focuses on an array of topics not only locally but internationally. It features up-and-coming style trends, influential bands, products you have to try, new places to hang out, spectacular shows and opinions from local writers. It prides itself on firsthand information only: interviews are a must and priority.

Photos by Maria Lujic Photography

Alma Natural Quick Spa

2105 Yonge St, Toronto, 416.546.7462
almanaturalspa.com, facebook.com/almanaturalspa, Twitter: @almanaturalspa

All-natural. Convenient. Unpretentious.
Alma Natural Quick Spa provides convenient services for the consumer who doesn't have the luxury of time to spend hours at the spa. Each service is enhanced by all-natural, handmade products. You can view the schedule and book appointments online as soon as 15 minutes from now! Check out their tea boutique for tea to stay or go, and take advantage of their free Wi-Fi.

Katie Grennan

Q&A

What do you like best about owning a business?
Getting to create something that has so much of me in it. And knowing that we put a smile on a customer's face.

How do you relax?
I find yoga to be really helpful, and a glass of red wine!

What place inspires you and why?
New York City inspires me because I truly feel every person can be him/herself, and the energy is unparalleled.

What do you CRAVE?
A time when I can read the ingredient lists on my food and personal care products and know what each ingredient is and that it is safe and natural.

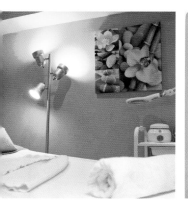

Alma Speaker Series

* "Natural Relief from Chronic Pain"
When: Nov. 10th 7:30 pm
Tickets: FREE visit us at www.almanaturalspa.com

* "Detoxify your Skin"
When: Nov. 16th 7:30 pm
Tickets: FREE visit us at www.almanaturalspa.com for more information!

Amalsroom.com

amalsroom.com, facebook.com/amalsroom, Twitter: @amalsroom

Bohemian. Ethnic. Eclectic.
Bringing some of the world's most unique, finest and exquisite treasures from across the globe, Amalsroom.com is an online destination for customers who want to find a unique gift—with bohemian chic flair—or simply treat themselves to an exotic indulgence. From spices and teas and home décor items, Amalsroom.com offers a wide array of home, body, fashion and gourmet foodie items.

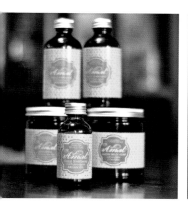

Amal Aflak

Q&A

What tip would you give women
who are starting a business?
Follow your dreams and gain thorough
knowledge of the industry that fuels your
passion before you spend any money. You are
likely to be your first and possibly only investor.

What do you like best about
owning a business?
Travelling to different parts of the world,
attending trade shows and shopping
for unique and artistic merchandise
to share with my customer fan base
and other individuals in the trade.

Who is your role model or mentor?
Manuela, a kind entrepreness, has no idea
that I have been looking up to her since
I met her a few years ago and Helen, my
Wall Street comrade and governess!

Bianca Sprague and
Natasha Marchand

Q&A

What do you like best about
owning a business?
The freedom of being your
own boss! If we need a day with
our daughters and spouses, then
we can take it. It is a real gift.

What motivates you on a daily basis?
We have grown so much that
it's not about just the two of us
anymore. We have a team of 24
behind us. They are great motivation.

What is your motto or theme song?
At any given moment, you have the
power to say: This is *not* how the story
is going to end. We have to keep going:
this story needs a better ending.

bebo mia inc.

416.363.2326, bebomia.com, facebook.com/bebomiainc, Twitter: @bebomia

Fresh. Informative. Supportive.

bebo mia is changing maternal health from the inside-out! Offering care from fertility through pregnancy and well into parenting, these pregnancy and parenting practitioners provide premium support and education. The bebo mia girls offer classes and services throughout Toronto, most done in the comfort of your own home. bebo mia really is a one-stop shop for all things pregnancy and baby!

bebo mia
fertility · pregnancy · parenting

Primary Doula
Direct Line

Secondary D
Direct Lin

LilyPadz®

1-800-640-LILY • www.lilypadz.com

THE CANADIAN BESTSELLER

Dr. Jack Newman's

GUIDE TO

BREASTFEEDING

❝Surround yourself with people who support you. Business is too hard to do alone—delegate as much as you can! It is all about community.❞

Bianca Sprague and Natasha Marchand of bebo mia inc.

Because You Said So...

647.927.4790, becauseyousaidso.net
facebook.com/BecauseYouSaidSo, Twitter: @becauseusaidso

Organized. Creative. Driven.
Because You Said So... (BYSS...) is a unique promotions and events company that combines 30 years of experience. BYSS... listens to what you want and creates a one-of-a-kind personal experience. BYSS... creates experiences that are very detailed while maintaining creativity. BYSS... strives to be flexible enough to take on any challenge but determined and organized enough to fit your budget. Let's plan your event!

Cathy and Brooke Milne

 # Q&A

What are your most popular products or services?
Event planning, personalized experiences, unique destination weddings, book and product launches, store openings.

What tip would you give women who are starting a business?
Cathy: Believe in yourself, work hard and have fun!
Brooke: Find your passion and run with it!

What motivates you on a daily basis?
Cathy: I love creating and working with my daughter. I love all the possibilities that exist.
Brooke: Creating one-of-a-kind events with my mom and engaging in social media.

What do you CRAVE?
Cathy: To make a difference!
Brooke: Change!

Paige Boersma

What tip would you give women who are starting a business?
Do your research and surround yourself with motivating people who can mentor and support you throughout the process. Also, passion is essential, and entrepreneurship isn't a career, it's a lifestyle!

What do you like best about owning a business?
The creative freedom it offers and the challenges that I'm faced with on a daily basis never cease to inspire me and push me to do better, which I love.

What place inspires you and why?
The shop itself is a constant source of inspiration. We're constantly brainstorming, designing displays and helping customers find the perfect outfit.

Bicyclette Boutique

880 Queen St W, Toronto, 416.532.8048
shopbicyclette.ca, facebook.com/bicycletteboutique, Twitter: @ShopBicyclette

Whimsical. Eclectic. Feminine.
Bicyclette Boutique offers a finely curated assortment of women's clothing, accessories, and beauty and gift items, drawing inspiration from a whimsical, nostalgic aesthetic and mixing it with a modern, downtown feel: street style meets fairy tale. Sourcing established international lines and mixing them with local designers, Bicyclette offers a rich selection and a lifestyle-specific shopping experience in an interactive and stimulating visual environment, online and in-store.

Blossom Lounge

157 Main St, Unionville, 905.479.8355
blossomlounge.com, blossomeveryday.blogspot.com
facebook.com/blossomlounge, Twitter: @blossomlounge

Trendsetting. Fashion-forward. Feminine.
Blossom Lounge was created in 2004 from Shauna Podruzny's frustration of not being
able to find many international bath, body and beauty product lines in the Canadian
market. Initially launching online, Blossom Lounge grew into a lifestyle boutique offering
many exclusive, hard-to-find beauty and fashion lines from around the world.

Photos by Sam and Duke

Shauna Podruzny

Q&A

What are your most popular products or services?
Beauty brands such as Kai Fragrance, Lollia and Butter London always see customers coming back for more and top clothing brands include Colcci, Mavi, Gentle Fawn and LA Made.

How do you relax?
I've learned to slow everything down in life and to stop rushing everything I do. By taking a step back, I've learned to make better decisions to better achieve goals.

What do you CRAVE?
I crave harmony; I love balance in my life. When something is off, it's hard to focus. When there's harmony, every day just feels perfect.

BISTROT DE PARIS

VINS DE BORDEAUX

> *"The best part of owning my business is being able to have total creative freedom at work every day."*
>
> Shauna Podruzny of Blossom Lounge

body blitz spa

471 Adelaide St W, Toronto, 416.364.0400
bodyblitzspa.com, facebook.com/bodyblitzspa, Twitter @bodyblitzspa

Rejuvenating. Modern. Sublime.

body blitz spa is a women's-only spa that puts a modern twist on ancient restorative water practices. Situated in an 11,000 sq. ft. warehouse space in the heart of Toronto, body blitz boasts a 38 ft. Dead Sea salt pool, hot green tea pool, cold plunging pool, aromatherapy steam, infrared sauna and 20 treatment rooms. Relax in therapeutic waters, detoxify in steam and sauna or replenish in mud, scrub, body or massage treatments. body blitz ~ health by water, ancient treatments, forward thinking.

Laura and Rena Polley

 # Q&A

What is the key to customer loyalty?
Great staff, excellent customer
service, consistency and making
your clients feel like they matter.

What are your signature
treatments or services?
Our body treatments include full-body
scrubs, muds and body glows. We use
our own line of body blitz products in our
treatments, and you can choose your own
mud or scrub from our scrub 'n mud bar.

What makes your business unique?
Our therapeutic water circuit. You can do the
circuit on its own or combine it with a treatment
for added benefit. And, of course, our own
argan oil. We are the only spa in Canada
to develop our own product line using the
amazing properties of Moroccan argan oil.

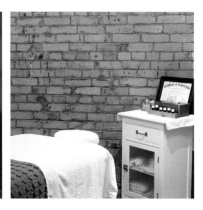

Photo by Jessica Lin Photography

" The best part is walking into the spa and seeing women of all ages, sizes, races and religions laughing, talking, lounging, using the waters and filling the place with humanity. "

Laura and Rena Polley of body blitz spa

Nicole Ritchie-Oseen

Q&A

What are your most popular products or services?
One of our best-selling styles are our Canadian-made Yoga Jeans. They are truly the most comfortable, and addictive, denim!

What tip would you give women who are starting a business?
Give your business time to grow and yourself time to learn!

What do you like best about owning a business?
The work I do is ultimately about making necessary changes to the fashion industry. I also simply adore helping women feel great about themselves! The clothes are the icing.

body politic

604.568.5528, bodypolitic.ca
facebook.com/bodypoliticboutique, Twitter: @body_politic

Emboldened. Lasting. Contemporary.

body politic began as a neighbourhood boutique in Vancouver, fulfilling the need for a well-curated selection of ethical and organic clothing and accessories. Quickly, demand stretched beyond the bricks-and-mortar store, resulting in the creation of an online storefront and customers stretching across North America. Today, body politic is a trusted source of the best contemporary eco-collections, satisfying its mandate of "sustainable design, limitless style."

Photos by Kari Heese

Cafe Novo

1986 Bloor St W, Toronto, 647.350.3538
cafenovo.ca, facebook.com/CafeNovo, Twitter: @cafenovo

Cozy. Organic. Bright.
Community-oriented, organic and fair-trade cafe and patisserie, featuring handmade goodies, baked in-house from certified organic, locally sourced ingredients.
Focusing on creating a warm, inviting atmosphere and serving lovingly crafted
lattes, cappuccinos and seasonal specialty drinks (hand-pressed lemonade
anyone?), Cafe Novo strives to be a neighborhood hub. With a tree-shaded, dog-
friendly patio. A perfect place to unwind with a good book or people watch.

Sadie Wilson and
Elizabeth Wimbush
(Melanie Hewson not pictured)

Q&A

What are your most popular products or services?
Our americanos are second to none, and our handmade cheesecake brownies are hard to pass up. Freshly steeped chai lattes are also very popular!

What tip would you give women who are starting a business?
Don't be afraid to ask for help, and take pride in every aspect of your business. Don't get discouraged easily—your hard work will pay off.

What is your motto or theme song?
"Well-behaved women rarely make history." —Laurel Thatcher Ulrich

What do you CRAVE?
Passion, laughter, balance and light. Oh, and the perfect night's sleep.

Diane Foisy Iannuzziello

 # Q&A

What are your most popular products or services?
Poems, vows, wedding stationery, addressed envelopes, place-seating cards, certificates, book inscriptions, speeches, eulogies, family trees and corporate event items.

What tip would you give women who are starting a business?
Do a survey to find out if your service or product is needed and wanted by the public. If there's a market, make yourself broadly known.

What do you like best about owning a business?
Flexibility of hours and no limit to the amount you want to make or to the size of business you want to have.

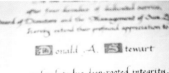

Calligraphy by Diane

By appointment only: 260 King St E, Ste A 408, Toronto, 416.518.1871
calligraphybydiane.com, diane@calligraphybydiane.com
Twitter: @calligraphybydi, facebook.com/calligraphybydiane
linkedin.com/in/calligraphybydiane, pinterest.com/calligrapher
bridaltweet.com/page/calligraphy-by-diane

Personalized. Beautiful. Artistic.
Calligraphy by Diane offers hand-done calligraphy in any lettering style and in
any language. With over 35 years of experience, Diane offers a 100 percent
guarantee that all work be beautiful, done perfectly and on time. Diane Foisy is
a perfectionist who insists that all of her work far exceeds expectations. It is that
level of service that has made her the most sought-after calligrapher. Diane's
published book and calligraphy kit, pictured on the left, is available for purchase.

The Cashmere Shop

24 Bellair St, Toronto, 416.925.0831
thecashmereshop.com, facebook.com/thecashmereshop, Twitter: @thecashmereshop

Contemporary. Timeless. Classic.
The Cashmere Shop is the original specialty shop for Cashmere in Toronto. In business
for almost 20 years, this boutique is a Toronto landmark. Sourcing only the very
best yarn, their cashmere is exclusively designed and knitted for the boutique.

Q&A

What are your most popular
products or services?
One of our most popular items is our wrap.

What do you like best about
owning a business?
I love that every day is different:
there is always something new.

What motivates you on a daily basis?
Doing better than the day before.

Who is your role model or mentor?
Retail maven Shirley Dawe. She taught
me to always evolve and take risks.

What is your motto or theme song?
"You only live once, but if you do it
right, once is enough." —Mae West

Alison Currie

❝ *Follow your intuition.* **❞**

Alison Currie of The Cashmere Shop

Christine Reid Photography

519.496.3857, christinereidphotography.com, Twitter: @creidphoto

Professional. Sincere. Real.

Christine Reid understands that the special moments in life need to be captured and therefore takes great pride in providing clients with high-quality photos that preserve these memories for years to come. Christine Reid Photography specializes in both wedding and portrait photography in the greater Toronto area but is also available for destination events worldwide.

Photos by Christine Reid Photography

Christine Reid

Q&A

What are your most popular products or services?
Our wedding photography packages are popular because they include a fun and candid engagement session that captures the couple in their favourite environment, being themselves, instead of stiff studio-like portraits.

What tip would you give women who are starting a business?
Remember why you started this path in the first place and never forget that. Always be inspired by your own vision and network with those who are doing the same.

What motivates you on a daily basis?
My clients, because without them I would not be where I am today. They believe in me from the beginning, so I absolutely have to come through for them.

Diana Howson (Owner) and Mika
Sato (Senior Design Manager)

Q&A

What tip would you give women
who are starting a business?
Say yes to the stress.

What do you like best about
owning a business?
Creative licence.

Who is your role model or mentor?
Jane Packer, a flower designer and
entrepreneur from London, UK.

What is your biggest fear?
Mediocrity.

What place inspires you and why?
Paris, Barcelona, the tropics,
mountains and wine valleys for their
natural and man-made beauty.

Coco & Lily Flowers Ltd

590 Markham St, Mirvish Village, Toronto, 416.537.2626
cocoandlilyflowers.com

Fresh. Upscale. Luscious.
Coco & Lily Flowers Ltd is a full-service shop creating bespoke floral designs for all occasions. This flower shop is welcoming and friendly and believes in cherishing its customers. Your flower order, whether it is a birthday, an international delivery, an event, wedding or funeral, gets our TLC always! Offering contemporary, stylish, beautiful flowers and second-to-none customer service—always!

Photos by Photography by Ardean, except portrait by IrinaPhotography

Q&A

What are your most popular products or services?
We are best known for our dresses and well-made suits. Our store staff gives one-on-one service with helpful advice that makes even the most reluctant shopper happy.

What tip would you give women who are starting a business?
The best advice we were given is to meet once a week and discuss business. A great idea is only great if you follow through and stay focused.

What motivates you on a daily basis?
Family, friends and the pleasure we get from the work that we do.

Judy Cornish and Joyce Gunhouse

Comrags

812 Dundas St W, Toronto, 416.360.7249
comrags.com, Twitter: @comrags

Urban. Unexpected. Timeless.
Comrags designers Joyce Gunhouse and Judy Cornish have created a well-loved line of women's clothing that has been described as "feminine despite themselves" and "prettiness with an edge." Their designs can be found in boutiques across Canada as well as in their flagship store in Toronto. Still made in-house, you can be sure of quality, which is reflected in their attention to detail and design.

Q&A

What tip would you give women who are starting a business?
Always trust your instinct. It will lead you in the right direction.

What is your motto or theme song?
"Success is liking yourself, liking what you do and liking how you do it." —Maya Angelou (b. 1928), author and poet

How do you relax?
Curling up on the couch with a Hollywood gossip magazine and a McDonald's McChicken combo.

What are your most popular products or services?
Definitely weddings and ribbon wrapping around vases, floral spheres and strung orchids.

What place inspires you and why?
Wholesaler's warehouses. Nothing compares to standing in a huge floral fridge. The smells, colour and textures transport me to a very blissful and inspiring place.

What do you CRAVE?
Laughter, integrity, Henry of Pelham Riesling, friendships, authenticity, a great pair of wedges, Spain (I have yet to get there!) and MAC cream blushes.

Shannon Jukes

CurlyGirl Flowers

289.259.5787, curlygirlflowers.com, Twitter: @CurlyGirlFlower

Fresh. Fancy. Fun.
The roses don't have to be red and the violets don't have to be blue when working with CurlyGirl Flowers. This floral design company focuses on unique colours and textures and designing with style, heart and flare. Their attention to detail has shaped their reputation for quality and their fun and friendly customer service brings enthusiasm and joy to your floral planning experience.

Photos by Ashley Watson Images

distill gallery

24 Tank House Lane, Ste 103, Toronto, 416.304.0033
distillgallery.com

Creative. Unique. Innovative.
distill was established in Toronto's Distillery District in 2003 with a mandate to
show individual handmade works by emerging Canadian artists/craftspeople/
designers contributing to contemporary material and visual culture. There is an
eclectic array of ceramics, glass, metalwork, woodwork and textiles. distill is
a destination for those who want something original and extraordinary.

Photos by Lemon Fresh Designs Photography

Allison Skinner

Q&A

What tip would you give women
who are starting a business?
My success as an entrepreneur stems
from being stubborn and passionate about
what I do—feed your passion, keep your
conviction and roll with the punches.

What do you like best about
owning a business?
Despite long hours and accounting,
distill energizes me. I'm inspired to see
what people make. There is no shortage
of talent and I want to support it.

What place inspires you and why?
Toronto. I love the energy of the city. There
is a vibrant arts and fashion scene here and
I feel fortunate to have direct access to that.

Rochelle Coleman and Lisa Ricciardelli

 Q&A

What are your most popular products or services?

Our online portal enables women to find support and connection during a critical time of need. Our business is becoming increasingly focused on live engagements, to talk through the practical approaches of the separation/divorce process.

What tip would you give women who are starting a business?

Be pragmatic and realistic, and enjoy the journey!

What do you like best about owning a business?

There is nothing more powerful than a female partnership in business ownership. We get to leverage who we are as women and—after coming from some of the largest global companies in the world—it feels great!

What motivates you on a daily basis?

Remaining true to the intention of Divorcegirlz Inc.

What place inspires you and why?

Paris, for the analogous combining of that which is history and that which Is new. And the wine is pretty good, too!

What do you CRAVE?

We crave providing women connection and support. Women making other women stronger.

Hey Sarah,
Heard about what happened!
Check out
www.DIVORCEGIRLZ.com.
it really helped me —
Joanne

Divorcegirlz Inc.

416.949.2371, divorcegirlz.com, Twitter: @divorcegirlz

Informed. Connected. Supportive.
Divorcegirlz Inc. are a group of women who have gone through the divorce
process from beginning to end. Finding clarity during this emotional time is a gift.
This portal seeks to ensure that you have the practical items that you need once
you've made the decision to move forward with separation and, ultimately, divorce.
Divorcegirlz Inc. provides connection to others in the same circumstance.

Upper-left photos by Adam Levett, portrait by Kira Crugnale, lower-right photo by Natasha V.

eLUXE

416.977.3325, eLUXE.ca, facebook.com/shopeluxe, Twitter: @shopeluxe

Stylish. Contemporary. Sophisticated.

Style connoisseurs rejoice! eLUXE is a premier Canadian online shopping site, offering the best in contemporary designer brands, expert tips and inspired looks in their online magazine, email notifications announcing new designers and products, and much more. eLUXE makes shopping easy with free shipping and returns, and no hidden duties or fees. Shopping from your home and native land has never looked so good!

Q&A

What are your most popular
products or services?
Popular brands include Smythe, Frye,
Pink Tartan, Foley + Corinna, Rebecca
Minkoff and J Brand. And everyone loves
our free shipping and free returns.

What tip would you give women
who are starting a business?
Being an entrepreneur is not for the faint of
heart! Things always take longer and cost more
than you anticipate. Be patient and persevere!

What do you like best about
owning a business?
The reward I feel of creating something out of
nothing. Knowing that every move we make
matters and that I get out as much as I put in.

Joanna Track

Photo by Natasha V.

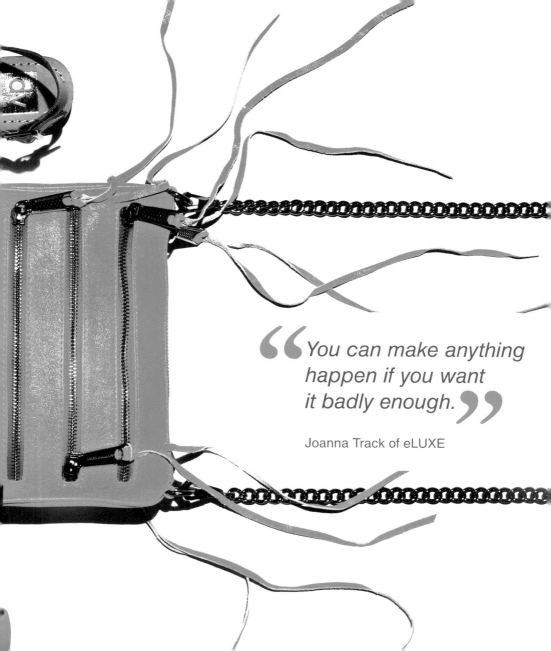

"You can make anything happen if you want it badly enough."

Joanna Track of eLUXE

Vivian Osal

Q&A

What are your most popular products or services?
An Integrated Session is a unique consultation combining a number of techniques such as intuitive guidance, meditation/hypnosis and energy healing to create a personalized deep-healing experience for the client.

What tip would you give women who are starting a business?
Set clear goals around your finances; create a business plan. Personal and business finances need to be managed separately right from the onset.

What motivates you on a daily basis?
I focus on the "feeling" I desire to experience. Knowing I am responsible for creating my own reality motivates me to create the beautiful life I want to live.

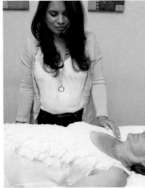

Evolving Being

By appointment only: 120 Eglinton Ave E, Ste 800, Toronto, 416.457.3330
osal.ca, Twitter: @vivianosal

Conscious. Healing. Balancing.
Vivian Osal is a spiritual teacher, counselor, intuitive channeler and energy healer.
She started her practice in 2000, and has assisted clients from all over the world
to discover and reconnect to the power of self-healing that lies within each of
us. Vivian guides individuals to connect with their authentic selves, ultimately
leading to more love, peace and joy in their personal and professional lives.

Feather Factory

1606 Queen St W, Toronto, 416.536.3391
featherfactory.com, facebook.com/featherfactory1, Twitter: @featherdivas

Eco-friendly. Creative. Unique.
Feather Factory customers are greeted with light, colour and texture. Rows of colourful quilts, cushions and sumptuous fine linens fill the boutique. Owners Cathy Bull, Martha Bull and Michelle Richardson have sourced unique brands in bed linens, towels and fabrics, and they make their own superior down products. Three Sisters Design is an exclusive line of bed linen that embraces their artistic influences. "Fine linens, down and designs for living."

Martha Bull, Michelle
Richardson and Cathy Bull

Q&A

What are your most popular products or services?
Our beautifully handcrafted down duvets and pillows. An in-house seamstress enables us to transform your ideas to one-of-a-kind room designs. Down refurbishing service.

Who is your role model or mentor?
We look up to all women entrepreneurs. We admire designers like Christiane Lemieux, founder of DwellStudio, Jane Hall Design, and Rosemary Carbonara of ro design.

What do you like best about owning a business?
The versatility, challenges and the freedom to express our creativity.

Esther Ha and Jennifer Yang

Q&A

What are your most popular products or services?
Our cakes and flowers, of course! Oh, and our cupcakes, too.

What tip would you give women who are starting a business?
Do what you love. Never underestimate the power of "word of mouth." Be very patient: with your clients, the people you work with and especially your business.

What do you like best about owning a business?
Having our clients turn into friends. We're there for a lot of their important milestones, and it really is great to be able to share those moments with them.

Flour Studio

883 Eglinton Ave W, Toronto, 416.789.0222
flourstudio.com

Lovely. Splendid. Delightful.
Flour Studio combines the best of both: a sweet little bakery and a beautiful
flower boutique. The baked goods are lovingly made from scratch daily with
premium all-natural ingredients. Floral events, whether for an elaborate
soiree or a simple table arrangement, are custom-designed with care.

Photos by by Maria Lalla Photography

Nadine Charbonneau

Q&A

What are your most popular products or services?
Our group fitness classes and personal training sessions. Our focus is on the mental and physical wellness of our women. We want smiles and sore muscles!

What tip would you give women who are starting a business?
Do what you love and are passionate about. Use your talents to create a successful business. Have faith in yourself, in your abilities and in your business.

What do you like best about owning a business?
The hard work it takes to build a business and the huge sense of accomplishment each day. I'm so thankful to be doing what I love to help women be their best.

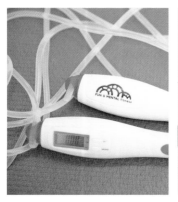

Fun & Mental Fitness

416.231.5432, funandmentalfitness.com
facebook.com/FunAndMentalFitness, Twitter: @FnMFitness

Surprising. Results-driven. Community-based.
Fun & Mental Fitness teaches the fundamentals of healthy living. Fundamentals you can use every day to feel better physically and mentally. It's not just about exercise, it's about how *you* can be a better mother, wife, sister, girlfriend, daughter and *woman*. Fun & Mental Fitness provides education and guidance on your inner self and fun workouts for your outer self. This is *not* a bootcamp.

Florence Gaven and Jessica Frampton

Q&A

What are your most popular products or services?
Our Fuzz Faithful Membership is a definite favorite among female clients. For just $35 a month, ladies get a Bikini, Sexy Bikini or Brazilian wax, plus plenty of perks.

What tip would you give women who are starting a business?
When starting out, don't be too proud to ask for help. You will be surprised at the number of people willing to lend a hand or give you a boost.

What motivates you on a daily basis?
We have big plans for Fuzz Wax Bar, and the desire to grow our business keeps us excited and motivated about what tomorrow will bring.

Lower-left photos by Christine Reid Photography

Fuzz Wax Bar

701 Queen St W, Toronto, 647.748.3899
fuzzwaxbar.com, facebook.com/FuzzWaxBar, Twitter: @FuzzWaxBar

Fast. Focused. Flawless.

Fuzz Wax Bar is Toronto's first wax bar and the downtown destination for looking fuzz-free and fabulous. Catering to both ladies and gents, this sassy and sophisticated shop is dedicated entirely to waxing. Their wax professionals provide superior service with minimal ouch factor—from head to toe and everything in between. Finally, a great wax at a good price and done quickly.

Georgie Porgie Cakes & Gifts

877-456-LOOT (877.456.5668), georgieporgie.ca
facebook.com/georgieporgiecreations, Twitter: @GPgiftqueen

Creative. Colourful. Delicious.

Georgie Porgie is a creative gift and cake house, creating one-of-a-kind custom cakes and cupcakes made from scratch with natural ingredients. The same love and care is put into every party loot bag, event favour and gift basket for your event or gift-giving needs to create a lasting impression for life's celebrations.

Photos by Photography by Ardean

Georgette Dehaney

Q&A

What tip would you give women
who are starting a business?
Never veer away from your passion.
Research, test it and make it better.
You can never learn too much about
what you want to do for a business.

What do you like best about
owning a business?
Customer service. Meeting with our clients
to unravel their visions; then making
those visions come to life and seeing
their happiness and appreciation.

What is your motto or theme song?
I didn't have one until one day my brother
hummed the song "The Eye of the
Tiger" to get motivated; after laughing
hysterically, I too now hum that tune.

Sandra Cowan

Q&A

What are your most popular products or services?
New digital lenses, RetroSuperFuture sunglasses from Italy.

What tip would you give women who are starting a business?
Never take no for an answer.

What do you like best about owning a business?
I always get the last word.

What place inspires you and why?
Amsterdam—if you have ever been, you know.

What do you CRAVE?
Peace in the Middle East and my own apartment with martinis on tap.

Goldstein Boutique

171½ King St E, Toronto, 416.368.9910
goldsteinboutique.com

Quirky. Stylish. Original.
Goldstein Boutique opened in 1998 to offer a unique personal eyewear experience. There are no walls of frames or harsh lighting, just the benefit of Sandra Cowan's 25 years of experience and international scouting of boutique brands and up-and-comers. This is a one-woman show—no juniors. Sandra just shares her creative eye for which of the 1000 frames is perfect for you.

Photos by Maria Lalla Photography

Grâce Toléqué

Q&A

What do you like best about owning a business?
Fulfilling a dream at this time of my life. I am doing what I love; how many people get to do that?

What is your motto or theme song?
From Maya Angelou: "When you know better, you do better." Wonderful words to live by, both in business and in life. They fuel my constant quest for knowledge.

What place inspires you and why?
Born in Paris, raised in Africa and North America in a family of diplomats, I am inspired by my travels, indigenous art, life experiences, love and African craftsmanship.

Grace & Angeline
Jewelry Studio

256 Durie St, Toronto, 416.546.5150
graceandangeline.com
facebook.com/graceandangelinejewelry, Twitter: @GraceNangeline

Timeless. Delicate. Elegant.

Grace & Angeline is a jewellery studio unlike any other. The intimate boutique offers stunning handcrafted jewellery in a warm yet chic setting. Each limited-edition design is lovingly crafted in high-quality sterling silver, gold-filled, or with 14- and 18-karat gold with luminous, hand-picked gemstones. The boutique also offers custom-design services to allow clients to take part in designing a jewel uniquely their own.

Photos by H2Photo

H2Photo

416.702.4165, h2photo.ca
facebook.com/h2photo.ca, Twitter: @hopehanson

Creative. Exciting. Personal.

H2Photo is a boutique photography studio nestled between Oakville and Mississauga, servicing the entire GTA. H2Photo specializes in capturing the moments that fill your life. Whether it is the first time the bride and the groom see each other or the arrival of a baby, H2Photo wants you to have these memories saved to enjoy for years to come.

Hope Hanson

Q&A

What are your most popular
products or services?
Our specialty is our one-year-old
portrait sessions called "Cake Smash."
That's right, add one toddler and one
cake, and watch the icing fly!

What tip would you give women
who are starting a business?
Be an expert in your field, have a strong
business sense and know when to delegate.

What do you like best about
owning a business?
I love being able to create my own hours and
work with amazing people and families.

> **"** *I crave good friends,*
> *family and lots of fun!* **"**
>
> Hope Hanson of H2Photo

Photo by H2Photo

Helga Teitsson

Q&A

What are your most popular
products or services?
From first-time home buyers to the empty
nester downsizing, I help to find the perfect
home or get it sold if it's time to move.

What tip would you give women
who are starting a business?
Be clear on what you want to
accomplish and what value you
bring to your clients, and take action
every day toward your goals.

What motivates you on a daily basis?
The warm and fuzzy way I feel when I
receive a beautiful testimonial. Knowing
that I don't work at a job but rather have
the opportunity to affect people's lives.

RE/MAX
Hallmark Realty Ltd., Brokerage*

Helga Teitsson
Piece by Piece. Step by Step. By your Side.
www.HelgasHomes.com
416-486-5588

FOR SALE

A Spectacular Unobstructed Lake View

HELGATEITSSON
BROKER

VISIT MY WEBSITE FOR A VIDEO TOUR OF THIS PROPERTY:
www.HelgasHomes.com

416.486.5588

RE/MAX
Hallmark Realty Ltd., Brokerage

RE/MAX®

Helga's Homes

723 Mt. Pleasant Rd, Toronto, 416.486.5588
helgashomes.com, facebook.com/HelgasHomes, Twitter: @helgashomes

Enthusiastic. Dynamic. Industrious.

Whether you are looking to buy or sell a condominium, single-family home or an income property, Helga will be there to direct and guide the entire process with expertise and finesse. The Toronto real estate market can be fast-paced and unpredictable, so it's essential to have an experienced realtor by your side. Take Helga with you on your next real estate adventure.

401 **QUEENS** WEST
SUITE 305

A Spectacular Unobstruc

HELGA TEITSSON

> **"** *I like being in control of my future, knowing that my success is directly related to my efforts, that the sky is the limit.* **"**

Helga Teitsson of Helga's Homes

I Heart Accessories

416.792.1271, iheartaccessories.ca
facebook.com/shopiheartaccessories, Twitter: @ihartaccessries

Fun. Fashionable. Charismatic.

I Heart Accessories features trendy jewellery and accessories for women who enjoy adding that extra little bit of style to their wardrobe. Their collection is specially curated by a fashion lover who handpicks each item with her customers in mind. Selections include fashion jewellery, bags, wallets, hats, scarves and tights that range from fun and funky to semiformal... Accessories from head to toe.

Photos by Lemon Fresh Designs Photography

Natalie Colalillo

Q&A

What tip would you give women
who are starting a business?
Make a decision to succeed even if some of
your plans fall through. A true entrepreneur
should be able to rise above whatever
challenges come her way and keep going.

What do you like best about
owning a business?
The fact that I have made my vision a
reality that I adore, and that I get to design
my own life on my own terms. Bliss.

What motivates you on a daily basis?
My vision. I know exactly where I am going. I
think of what my life will look like in five years
if I just keep going, and it looks pretty sweet.

What is your motto or theme song?
Raise the bar. If you can see
it, it's not high enough.

ideal samples Inc.

416.871.3241, idealsamples.com, Twitter: @idealsamples

Passionate. Expert. Results-driven.
Ideal Samples helps you bring your ideas to life and to market. They are your team of experts, working with you through every step of the process, giving you the tools, resources and support you need to achieve your goals and dreams faster.

Q&A

What tip would you give women who are starting a business?
Get clarity on your big vision and own it. Surround yourself with amazing like-minded women who can help make that reality.

What do you like best about owning a business?
I love the freedom to challenge the status-quo—improving the way entrepreneurs do business.

What motivates you on a daily basis?
Incredible women with big ideas who are pushing the limits and making s*it happen!

What is your motto or theme song?
Believe anything is possible and be amazing.

Sheena Repath

in2art Gallery

Gallery hours: Wednesday–Saturday 10am–4pm and by appointment
350 Lakeshore E, Ste 1B, Oakville, 905.582.6739
in2artgallery.com, Twitter: @in2artoakville

Contemporary. Urban. Funky.
A fresh take on the gallery experience, in2art takes the pretension and the anxiety out of buying original art. Fast becoming the "west end source for art," owners Kelly and Susan have selected a unique group of contemporary artists giving the collection a design-forward and urban feel. With over 70 artists, they feel anyone can and should own original art.

Photos by Maria Lalla Photography

Q&A

What are your most popular products or services?
We spend a lot of time in clients' homes, helping them source and place the perfect piece of art, at no added cost. Our clients love this service!

What tip would you give women who are starting a business?
Patience... it takes time to build your name and credibility, so never underestimate the power of word of mouth, social media and the support of friends and family.

What place inspires you and why?
Interior design magazines! We love looking at how people live and what art they have on their walls.

Kelly McDonagh and
Susan Hoeltken

" *The best part of owning a business is complete creative control... in a business like art, we think clients want us to show them what is new, what is exciting, who is up and coming.* **"**

Kelly McDonagh and Susan
Hoeltken of in2art Gallery

Wendy Crystal

Q&A

What tip would you give women
who are starting a business?
Stay positive and collaborate with others.
Networking is one of best business-
building opportunities around.

What do you like best about
owning a business?
Inspiring people. Seeing my ideas
become a reality. Helping women
to feel good about themselves and
to create a career within Inspire.

What motivates you on a daily basis?
Inspiring women, knowing the love women
have for my products and how in a few
short minutes, we change women's lives.

Photos by Christine Reid Photography

Inspire Cosmetics

212 - 150 Lakeshore Rd W, Mississauga, 416.827.8504
inspirecosmetics.com, Twitter: @Inspirecosmetic

Inspiring. Innovative. Customizable.
Founded by Ford model Wendy Crystal, Inspire Cosmetics is a high-quality cosmetics
line at affordable prices. Vitamin-enriched formulas, SPF protection, fragrance-free
and hypo-allergenic products for every woman. Customize the line you desire with
Inspire. Simple selection and easy application. You don't need to be a pro to know
how to get flawless, breathable skin in just a few minutes. Consultant opportunities.

Irina Fortey

Q&A

What tip would you give women who are starting a business?
As a business undergraduate, I found that having business fundamentals really helped me establish a strong direction for my business. Engage in learning through business courses: knowledge is power.

What is your motto or theme song?
There is always time to get things done, sometimes it's all about your priorities.

What do you CRAVE?
There is a synergy between my photography and my life. My passion is my craft and I want others to know that I put my heart into my work.

IrinaPhotography

647.218.2440, irinaphotography.ca
facebook.com/IrinaPhotography, Twitter: @irinafortey

Authentic. Vibrant. Joyful.
IrinaPhotography is a boutique photography studio in the heart of downtown,
offering memorable experiences with each artistic and contemporary portrait
session. Clients appreciate the creative and soulful imagery created of their families.
The product line is filled with beautifully designed prints, collages, storyboards,
custom cards and heirloom albums that tell the unique story of each capture.

Photos by IrinaPhotography

Jessica Lin Photography

416.806.1585, jessicalin.ca, Twitter: @jessicalinphoto

Personal. Genuine. Priceless.
Jessica Lin is passionate about capturing the beauty of relationships, objects and places. When she and her husband Norman aren't photographing important life moments such as weddings or new babies, she's capturing the latest pieces created by her artist and designer clients for their portfolios. Jessica is also currently working on a series of multimedia art pieces incorporating her travel and personal photographic images.

 Q&A

What are your most popular products or services?
Custom albums and artwork. My clients love the gorgeous one-of-a-kind pieces I make for them.

What tip would you give women who are starting a business?
Love what you do: it will show.

Who is your role model or mentor?
My moms—Kezia, Joanne and Julie—all of whom have a fearless entrepreneurial spirit.

What place inspires you and why?
I love travelling and experiencing new places: the colours, textures, language and history are an endless source of fascination and inspiration for me.

Jessica Lin

Kathleen Kohut

Q&A

What tip would you give women who are starting a business?
Stay completely focused on your vision. Take advice and constructive criticism and apply it as needed. Talk to others going through the same and believe in you... always.

What place inspires you and why?
There are women's shelters in Toronto that I have visited to volunteer at and donate clothing. The women remind me what real strength is and that I can keep on, too!

What do you CRAVE?
Seeing women exude more confidence after a wardrobe makeover and having the realization that clothes are one thing, but who they really are is inside all along.

Kathleen's Closet

kathleen@kathleenscloset.com, kathleenscloset.com, Twitter: @KathleensCloset

Modern. Affordable. Fun.

Kathleen's Closet offers a unique and affordable wardrobe consultation service, based in Liberty Village, Toronto, that also hosts fun events to gather clothing for women in need or for those living in shelters.

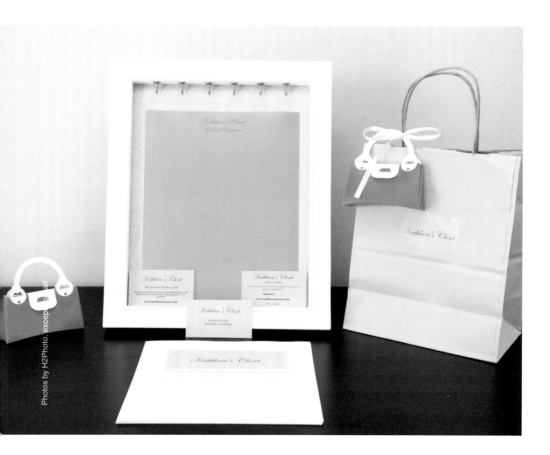

Kathryn L. Smithen
Barrister, Solicitor & Notary Public

27 Yorkville Ave, Ste 201, Toronto, 416.925.2123
kathrynsmithen.ca

Approachable. Thoughtful. Thorough.
Kathryn L. Smithen runs a law practice that focuses exclusively on family law issues. She particularly enjoys representing women and children. Kathy went to law school as a mature student, a single parent of a teenager and a self-represented family law litigant. She is particularly sensitive to and recognizes the struggle that some moms and kids face when looking for access to affordable justice.

Q&A

What tip would you give women who are starting a business?
You teach people how to treat you by what you tolerate. Trust your instincts. Don't let other people define you. You are entitled to your share of the proverbial pie.

Who is your role model or mentor?
All the women who came before me and made it possible for me to be a mother and a lawyer without having to sacrifice either role or apologize for my choices.

What is your motto or theme song?
Determination is stronger than fear. My other favourite saying is "you can't scare me. I have children."

Kathryn (Kathy) Smithen

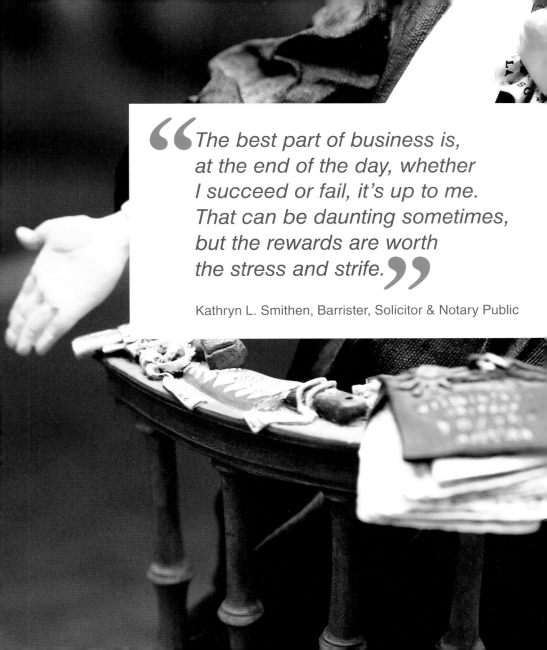

> **"** *The best part of business is, at the end of the day, whether I succeed or fail, it's up to me. That can be daunting sometimes, but the rewards are worth the stress and strife.* **"**

Kathryn L. Smithen, Barrister, Solicitor & Notary Public

Kerr Street Cafe

298 Kerr St, Oakville, 289.837.1535
Kerr Street Cafe North: 96 Joseph St, Port Carling, 289.837.1535
kerrstreetcafe.com, facebook.com/KerrStreetCafe, Twitter: @kerrstreetcafe

Flye Catering

298 Kerr St, Oakville, 416.519.9023
flyecatering.com, Twitter: @flyecatering

Fresh. Creative. Local.
Kerr Street Cafe was the next logical step for Flye Catering. Alex has been catering for 20 years throughout the GTA and Muskoka. Alex and her partner wanted to create a cafe where everyone could enjoy the food they are so passionate about. With a love for flavors, presentation and creative menus, the Kerr Street Cafe is a delightful and relaxing meeting place.

Photos by Christine Reid Photography

Q&A

What are your most popular products or services?
The best coffee in Oakville! Breakfast and lunches that are healthy, fresh and delicious. And a wide range of prepared frozen meals ready to go.

What tip would you give women who are starting a business?
Have confidence and follow your passion. Start slow and don't spend money unnecessarily. Substitute creativity for deep pockets. Be invested for the long term and persevere!

How do you relax?
I love cooking for family and friends. Spending time with those whom I care about and enjoying delicious food and great conversation is what life is all about.

Alexandra Flye

Jeanette Aro

Q&A

What are your most popular products or services?
We are best known for our Luxe Moments women-only events, and our Escapeto Travel Lifestyle program that provides opportunity to experience the most authentic products/ services in a selected destination.

Who is your role model or mentor?
I admire women of influence like Oprah Winfrey, Dr. Pat Francis and Michelle Obama.

What place inspires you and why?
The beautiful island of Barbados inspires me with its white beaches and awesome sunsets. I love the people, its food and culture. It is a must-see!

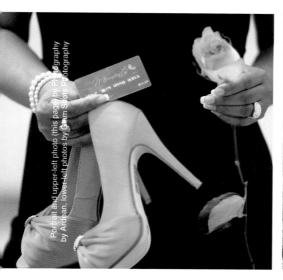

Kharisma Luxe Inc.

800.747.0672, kharismaluxe.com, Twitter: @kharismaluxe

Luxe Moments Lifestyle

800.747.0672, luxemoments.com, Twitter: @luxemoments

Escapeto Travel Lifestyle

800.747.0672, escapetocard.com, Twitter: @escapetocard

Extravagant. Unique. Dynamic.
Kharisma Luxe is an elite experience aggregator that has given birth to two niche luxury, lifestyle and experience marketing programs: the Luxe Moments Lifestyle for women, and Escapeto Travel Lifestyle for travellers, which are built on loyalty and incentive solutions to connect businesses and consumers more effectively.

Mt Meikle

Q&A

What tip would you give women who are starting a business?
Follow your passion, find creative ways to deal with challenges and obstacles, be persistent and remember the value of networking.

What do you like best about owning a business?
I love the independence and self-expression, being my own boss, being able to pursue my passion, feeling more confident and focused, and continual learning.

Who is your role model or mentor?
Jeanne Beker and Rachel Zoe. Both these women have reinvented themselves multiple times and have successful fashion businesses while being truly authentic.

la closette

647.223.2992, laclosette.com, facebook.com/laclosetteMT, Twitter: @laclosette_MT

Resourceful. Visionary. Authentic.
la closette is a network for professional advice, insider fashion and wellness resources, specifically for savvy women wanting to look current and fashion forward. They offer image consulting and workshops on dressing for your lifestyle and wardrobe analysis. Bringing women support and guidance to be accessibly stylish, la closette wants you to love what you wear and feel confident! The fashion market hub for introducing and sourcing new, exciting designs.

Lilliput Hats

462 College St, Toronto, 416.536.5933
lilliputhats.com, facebook.com/lilliputhats, Twitter: @lilliputhats

Bespoke. Handmade. Sculptural.
Lilliput Hats is Toronto's only full-service traditional millinery. Celebrating over
two decades in business, Lilliput Hats is a go-to place for fine hats, headpieces,
bridal as well as casual, practical styles. Each Lilliput Hat is handmade
on-site from the finest materials, and styles are added weekly. Designer
Karyn Ruiz and her charming staff can help you select the perfect hat!

Karyn Ruiz

What tip would you give women
who are starting a business?
Talk to other women whose business you
admire. Network as much as you can
and don't be afraid to make mistakes.

What do you like best about
owning a business?
I make decisions that I am accountable for,
and I can craft the kind of life that I want.

What motivates you on a daily basis?
I design beautiful creations for interesting
and eclectic individuals. Every day someone
says thank you to me. I employ and work
alongside funny, intelligent and quirky women.

What is your motto or theme song?
No one ever regretted buying quality.

Lolobeauty

416.708.8613, lolobeauty.net
facebook.com/MYLOLOBEAUTY, Twitter: @mylolobeauty

Unique. Chic. Glamourous.
Let her be a spa princess, rock-star diva or glamour girl for the day! Known for creating chic
girl-inspired party experiences, Lolobeauty turns ordinary parties into ultrafabulous events.
They provide several signature party packages and offer services that include pamper
treatments, designory stations, makeovers and hairstyling, all complete with upscale decor.
And best of all, the glitz and glam comes to you! They truly celebrate her and her and her...

Photos by H2Photo

Lorraine Lord

Q&A

What are your most popular products or services?
Our signature Pampered Princess Spa Party. Girls receive manicures with warm towel treatments, yummy pedicures and fruity facials with a makeover finale. Who doesn't love to be pampered!

What tip would you give women who are starting a business?
Continue to immerse yourself in knowledge about your industry and surround yourself with like-minded people. Awareness brings success!

What do you like best about owning a business?
Being able to bring my ideas from concept to reality. It's truly freeing to see your passions and dreams come to life.

Q&A

What tip would you give women who are starting a business?
We all need to remember that we are capable of doing way more than we think we can.

What do you like best about owning a business?
I love moving to the beat of my own drum. For me, this is the ultimate freedom.

What place inspires you and why?
I love Amsterdam. Quaint and cobbled streets with bikes going by, merchants quietly sweeping their front walks, welcoming in the day. The vibe is amazing, truly!

Sarah Dougall

Photos by Maria Lalla Photography

Made You Look

Made You Look Jewellery: 1338 Queen St W, Toronto, 416.463.2136
Made You Look Accessories: 1273 Queen St W, Toronto, 416.516.9595
madeyoulook.ca

Eclectic. Inspirational. Real.
Made You Look is a top destination for amazing, local designer jewellery.
Representing over 100 artists, Made You Look specializes in high-end custom work,
using rare and precious materials as well as the world's most unusual and creative
costume jewellery and "art to wear." With 20 resident designers creating on-site, Made
You Look offers every type of service including repairs, alterations and restorations.

MANE TEEZE by T&M Hair Perfume

2594 Yonge St, Toronto, 416.996.5000
maneteeze.com, Twitter: @mane_teeze

Delicious. Flirty. Desirable.

MANE TEEZE by T&M comes in three scents: Black Widow, Social Butterfly and Haut Mess, all of which aim to freshen the hair, invigorate the spirit and unlock the inner diva at any hour of the day. MANE TEEZE leaves a long-lasting fresh flavor to hair for up to 12 hours. Available in a fashionable glass bottle, easily toted in your gym bag or purse.

Q&A

What are your most popular products or services?
Our delicious line of premium hair perfume.

What tip would you give women who are starting a business?
Know that anything is possible. With an open mind and a positive attitude, success is in your future!

What do you like best about owning a business?
The freedom to be where you want when you want, to be creative every day and to build a chick's empire!

What motivates you on a daily basis?
Our goal and aspiration of creating a worldwide product keeps our butts in gear!

Tara McIntyre and Melanie Groom

Eleonora Caldato

Q&A

What are your most popular products or services?
Pizza, pasta and a great time, always!

What do you like best about owning a business?
Being my own boss and great satisfaction in doing what I am passionate about.

What is your motto or theme song?
You don't have to win every battle, make sure you win the war.

What place inspires you and why?
Any kitchen. There you see passion in action, discover new ingredients, cooking techniques, presentations. It's like being at a *great* concert!

MANGIA & BEVI resto-bar

260 King St E, Toronto, 416.203.1635
mbresto.com

Urban. Casual. Authentic.

MANGIA & BEVI is anything but standard! They create fresh foods inspired by
a contemporary urban Italian-style, prepared with a focus on seasonal, organic
and homemade products. Every day they serve fresh, intriguing and tasteful
Euro-style presentations with a splash of the Mediterranean and other regional
Italian influences. MANGIA & BEVI is located just east of the downtown core.

Photos by Christine Reid Photography

Mari Plawiuk Designs

mariplawiukdesigns.com, Twitter: @MariPDesigns

Authentic. Unique. Eclectic.
Mari Plawiuk Designs creates unique jewelry lines for retail clients and has been
in business for more than eight years. Her designs are showcased in exhibits
and her jewelry is sold in many boutiques and shops across Toronto and the
surrounding area. She has a devoted following of all ages and backgrounds,
including teenagers, businesswomen, artists and TV personalities.

Photos by Maria Lalla Photography

Mari Plawiuk

Q&A

What are your most popular
products or services?
We partner with boutique clients to create
exclusive jewelry designs that complement
the clothing lines they carry, offering their
clients diverse lines of versatile, well-
made jewelry to complement an outfit.

What do you like best about
owning a business?
Making things happen quickly without
restrictions and roadblocks—and having
the flexibility to prioritize my life in a way
that works for me and my family.

What motivates you on a daily basis?
My main motivations are delighting my clients
and knowing that my jewelry allows women to
express their personality through my designs.

Maria Lalla

Q&A

What tip would you give women who are starting a business?
Passion in what you do is always important, coupled with strong business skills. Ensure you have a well-thought-out business plan and be a connector, not a networker.

What do you like best about owning a business?
Being passionate about what I do and my commitment to fulfilling clients' needs, which in turn creates a satisfied client. Working with a variety of clients and situations.

What do you CRAVE?
To make a difference either locally or globally through bringing awareness with photography and helping other entrepreneurs, as I'm an avid public speaker, also.

Maria Lalla Photography

647.453.7453, marialalla.com, facebook.com/MMariaLalla, Twitter: @Maria_Lalla

Lalla Studios

647.453.7453, lallastudios.com, facebook.com/MMariaLalla, Twitter: @Maria_Lalla

Creative. Professional. Reflective.
Maria Lalla Photography specializes in photography for commercial, publicity, portfolio or personal needs. Working together with clients on business marketing and advertising needs, reflecting client's vision and brand. Lalla Studios provides wedding and portrait photography services.

Photos by Maria Lalla Photography

" I love the interaction with clients and the opportunity to creatively bring out their unique vision through images. "

Maria Lalla of Maria Lalla Photography and Lalla Studios

Meditative Arts

meditativearts.ca, facebook.com/MeditativeArts, Twitter: @meditativearts

Exotic. Soulful. Empowering.

Meditative Arts is where women, rhythm and bliss mingle! This unique rhythm and wellness program is said to be one of Toronto's best-kept secrets. Through African drumming and mindfulness courses, women are able to let go, have fun and find their inner rhythm. The "I can't stay still" and "I have NO rhythm" types are especially welcomed.

Q&A

What tip would you give women
who are starting a business?
Go with your gut and always keep
the bigger picture in mind.

What do you like best about
owning a business?
Freedom to choose how I'd like to lead my tribe.

What is your motto or theme song?
Authenticity trumps all.

How do you relax?
Drumming, meditating and lots of belly laughs!

What do you CRAVE?
People doing what they love at least once a
day... and, of course, tea and chocolate!

Michelle Currie

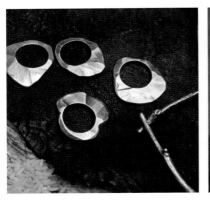

Melanie LeBlanc

Q&A

What are your most popular products or services?
Personalized, stacking bangles and stacking rings. My client is a confident woman who likes to create her own narrative, appreciates craftsmanship and wants to know the maker.

What tip would you give women who are starting a business?
Start small, challenge yourself, be competitive and take risks! Ask yourself: What sets me apart from the rest? Why do I want to do this?

What motivates you on a daily basis?
The awareness that I am solely responsible for my own success and destiny.

Melanie LeBlanc

647.427.4468, melanieleblanc.com

Mindful. Sculptural. Provocative.
With an extensive education in the visual arts, Melanie works exclusively
on running her business, established in 2003. She designs and handcrafts
every item produced. She currently works out of a studio gallery with
metalsmiths alike in Toronto's colourful west end. She also exhibits and
sells her work at juried craft shows, galleries and fine boutiques.

Photo by Jessica Lin Photography

Shannon Doyle

Q&A

What are your most popular products or services?
We've a stunning selection of fair trade, organic, local and handmade chocolates. As for popular: Fever Tree drinks, pumpkin fudge (seasonal), spices and rubs, and everything to make a fancy cupcake!

Who is your role model or mentor?
The best role models and mentors are people who support and encourage you. My mother has been a driving force behind me. But my entire family helped me to succeed.

What motivates you on a daily basis?
Customers say The Mercantile is artful, almost curated: finding exciting products for my customers really motivates me! Customers get excited too: there's always something new on display!

The Mercantile

297 Roncesvalles Ave, Toronto, 416.531.7563
themercantile.ca, facebook.com/themercantile.specialtyfoodsandtreats

Gourmet. Unique. Delicious.

A specialty food and treats shop, The Mercantile is chockablock full with unique and delicious foods. When you enter the store, you feel inspired, indulged and nurtured. The Mercantile is also a gift basket company beyond compare. Gift baskets are personally designed with each idiosyncratic recipient's needs in mind. The Mercantile: creating unique gift baskets for unique people since 1999.

Mildred & Doris Gift Studio

mildredanddoris.ca, Twitter: @mildredanddoris

Fresh. Friendly. Reliable.

Mildred & Doris Gift Studio is an online shop for picking and sending that "little something" to a friend. Be it a thumbs-up on a pregnancy announcement or a pick-me-up on a breakup, they have gifts that are as unique and special as her. Studio services also include corporate gift giving for businesses that primarily serve a female-client base.

Melanie Minor

Q&A

What are your most popular products or services?
Unique hand made vintage jewelry—the pieces are that perfect "little something" at a price point that is accessible. Customers also really enjoy creating care packages with bath soaps, fun chick-lit books and cute bath caps.

What tip would you give women who are starting a business?
Be bold. Ask for what you want. Don't let rejection impact your goals—look at why you were rejected, improve yourself, and move on. Seek constructive input from friends and family, but at the end of the day trust your instincts and follow your own star.

What motivates you on a daily basis?
The trust that my clients place in me is a true motivator to continue to do well and strive to do better.

Tasha Richard

Q&A

What are your most popular products or services?
Definitely our live in-city events having smart and savvy speakers, hot lattes, free childcare, great connections, stellar swag bags, and if we do our job right, moms leave feeling inspired!

What tip would you give women who are starting a business?
Planning and patience are your most powerful tools. And just when you think you have done enough business development, keep going!

What do you like best about owning a business?
I would be lying if I didn't say control: both over my time, and on how the brand is built and how we hope it is consumed!

momcafé
Network Inc.

877.MOM.7079 (877.666.7079), momcafenetwork.com
facebook.com/momcafenetwork, Twitter: @momcafenetwork

Professional. Inspiring. Authentic.
momcafé is a platform for authentic, open and honest conversations among
professional moms. They start the conversation with live events and continue
online with social media and professional development. Their mission is
connecting and inspiring professional moms along their professional journey.
momcafé is in several Canadian cities and is continuing its expansion in Canada
and in the United States via its licensing program for professional moms.

Photos by Jessica Rae Photography

Morris Feng Shui

416.899.7082, morrisfengshui.com
facebook.com/MorrisFengShui, Twitter: @morrisfengshui

Balanced. Harmonious. Peaceful.
Using a blend of traditional and intuitive Feng Shui, Laura Morris works closely with her clients to revitalize their living spaces to create balance and postive chi. As a certified Feng Shui consultant and interior decorator, she uses her knowledge of space planning, colour theory and Feng Shui to assess a space. Her services include one-on-one residential Feng Shui consultations, group workshops, colour consultations and space planning.

Photos by Maria Lalla Photography

Laura Morris

Q&A

What are your most popular products or services?
The Feng Shui Party: a two-hour in-home workshop. Feng Shui 101 for you and your friends. It makes a great girls' night.

What tip would you give women who are starting a business?
Find your passion, do your homework and take it a day at a time.

Who is your role model or mentor?
My grandmother. She was gracious, hardworking and all class.

What is your motto or theme song?
"Simplicity, patience, compassion. These three are your greatest treasures." —Lao Tzu

MSC Fitness

2480 Gerrard Ave E, Toronto, 416.686.3545
mscfitness.com, Twitter: @mscfitness

Innovative. Fun. Empowering.

MSC Fitness is a very cool, unique fitness studio in the Beaches, offering more than
60 innovative classes a week. Classes include spin, yoga (hatha, power, Vinyasa, Yin,
therapy), Pilates, kettlebells, weights, Bosu, aerial yoga, TRX, ultimate conditioning,
Just Backs and Fusion (SPOGA, cycle/sculpt). It is your best choice for total-body
fitness and well-being. A fun environment filled with people just like you.

Q&A

What tip would you give women who are starting a business?
Read all your contracts carefully. Read the fine print. Never personally guarantee anything.

Who is your role model or mentor?
I have a great friend Cynthia Funk, who owns all the Yoga Sanctuarys. We aim to be as organized and connected as Cynthia.

How do you relax?
Taking somebody else's yoga class, paddleboarding (we are now giving yoga classes on the boards), reading drinking nice wine with friends.

What do you CRAVE?
To be able to still be learning and teaching many years from now.

Charlene Sullivan and
Gudrun Hardes

Photo by Lemon Fresh Designs Photography

"Watching people change and become fitter and healthier as they learn more about their bodies motivates us.**"**

Charlene Sullivan and Gudrun
Hardes of MSC Fitness

Nancy Falconi

Q&A

What tip would you give women
who are starting a business?
Tune into and follow your intuition,
no matter what (what is essential
is invisible to the eye). Go for it!
(Leap, and the net will appear.)

What do you like best about
owning a business?
Unlimited potential for what I
can accomplish, create and
earn. No glass ceiling.

Who is your role model or mentor?
Women who are feminine, powerful and
not afraid to be different: Artemis, Isis,
Georgia O'Keeffe, Maria Montessori,
Louise Hay, Oprah, Cheryl Richardson.

Nancy Falconi Inc

416.992.9087, nancyfalconi.com
facebook.com/nfalconiinc, Twitter: @nancyfalconi, linkedin.com/in/NancyFalconi

Authentic. Uplifting. Sensitive.
Nancy Falconi is a visual and film artist, author and educator. She has the ability to look at her subject and capture its essence in an instant. The intent of her work is to raise awareness for self-love. Her work helps others to see that the deeper you go into yourself and the more personal you make your life, the more universal it becomes.

Photos by Nancy Falconi

nicenook

426.357. 9344, nicenook.com
facebook.com/nicenook, Twitter: @nicenook

Sustainable. Expressive. Personal.
nicenook is an online shop specializing in sustainable design services, furniture and home accents. Nicenook carries a mix of art deco, midcentury and industrial home furnishings. Reflecting on what you like, feel and sense of the world is crucial to decorating. nicenook's design services help clients create their ultimate nook. Offering unique, expressive and stylish home decor, nicenook helps you live your happiest, at home!

Q&A

What are your most popular products or services?
Our selection of Murano lamps, Scandinavian-inspired decor items and vintage dressers. And our two-hour redecorating package for $100.

What tip would you give women who are starting a business?
To differentiate yourself clearly from your competitors, you must surprise your customer. Don't create what the market needs or wants, create what it would *love*. Follow your imagination.

What is your motto or theme song?
You've got to let go of the good to get to the great.

Colleen Imrie

Marina Cortese

Q&A

What are your most popular
products or services?
In-home nutrition consults. Grocery store
tours. Corporate chats. Group workshops.

What do you like best about
owning a business?
Being accountable to myself and to my
clients. I'm my own boss and that's both
empowering and scary. Also, being able
to work in my bathrobe is a nice perk.

Who is your role model or mentor?
My mum. She's this tiny spitfire
and the strongest and smartest
lady I know! I wouldn't be half the
woman I am today without her!

What place inspires you and why?
My kitchen. That's where the magic (and
the occasional disaster) happens.

Nour-ish

647.822.3537, nour-ish.ca, facebook.com/benourished, Twitter: @nour_ish

Fresh. Fun. Tasty.

Nour-ish provides a refreshing way to take the plunge into eating right and getting healthy. Marina, holistic nutritionist and food lover, works with clients to improve their relationship with food and educates them about the foods that nurture the body and correct imbalances. Nour-ish is dedicated to restoring balance and health, making life a little bit easier, more enjoyable and delicious!

Upper middle and right photos (opposite page) by Maria Lalla Photography. Main photo (this page), portrait and upper left photos (opposite page) by Christine Reid Photography.

nour-ish.

nourishing from the root to the fruit

MARINA CORTESE
B.K fin, R.H.N, NNCP
TORONTO, ONT
EMAIL: MARINA@NOUR-ISH.CA
WEBSITE: WWW.NOUR-ISH.CA
PHONE: (647) 822.3537

Photo by Christine Reid Photography

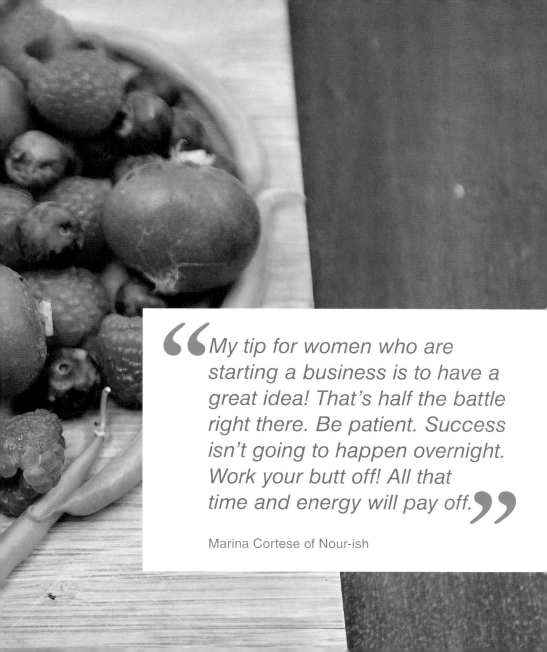

"My tip for women who are starting a business is to have a great idea! That's half the battle right there. Be patient. Success isn't going to happen overnight. Work your butt off! All that time and energy will pay off."

Marina Cortese of Nour-ish

Ohhh Canada

647.288.1118, ohhhcanada.ca, facebook.com/ohhhcanada, Twitter: @ohhh_canada

Sexy. Luxurious. Fashion-forward.

Ohhh Canada is the Canadian fashionista's favourite online boutique for sex toys, burlesque-style lingerie and sexy beauty products. Every product is hand-selected by Ohhh's staff to ensure that it's safe to use on your body and is the very best in its category. Well known for their second-to-none customer service, Ohhh's dedicated staff will help you find exciting ways to express your sexual side.

Photos by Aron Goss, Calculated Style Photography

Katrina McKay

Q&A

What are your most popular products or services?
Luxury vibrators that are beautiful to look at and oh-so-fun to play with. Best-in-class couples' sex toys. Girly-girl-approved burlesque-style panties, bustiers and lashes; plus gifts for him, too!

What tip would you give women who are starting a business?
You are your very first investor. Invest your money, invest your time, invest whatever you have; invest in yourself. Be prepared to lose, but plan to win. Take a risk.

What do you CRAVE?
Success as I define it, red wine, steak, sex and travel (not necessarily in that order). I have an insatiable appetite for the last two. Really, I do!

Janet Lewis

Q&A

What are your most popular products or services?
We love products that are interchange-able. Our most popular item is the Lotus Ring—a chic sterling silver ring with 30 marbles to match any outfit in your closet.

What do you like best about owning a business?
I like the freedom, flexibility and diversity. Every day brings different successes and challenges, making owning a business interesting and fun.

What do you CRAVE?
I crave the hunt! I love finding great new products that will surprise and delight others. There is nothing more exciting than seeing that look on someone's face.

Orangefish

416.607.6766, orangefish.ca
facebook.com/Orangefish.ca, Twitter: @Orangefish_, pinterest.com/orangefish01

Fabulous. Fresh. Fun.
Orangefish offers fabulous fresh finds for busy professionals, moms and fashionistas who are looking for that perfect gift or unique treat for themselves. Their aim is to provide members with products that set them apart from the crowd and allow them to shine. Orangefish features the hottest new fashion and lifestyle items from the comfort of your own home or office. They also offer corporate, event and fundraising programs.

" *Don't wait until everything is perfect to launch. Your business will evolve over time. Get feedback on how to improve and be willing to adapt based on this feedback.* **"**

Janet Lewis of Orangefish

Ardean Peters

Q&A

Who is your role model or mentor?
Anna Kuperberg, a wedding photographer in the San Francisco Bay area, and people who, despite having jobs, family, etc., still make time to follow their heart and do what they love.

What is your motto or theme song?
"Moving on up... Nothing can stop me... Time to break free!" That song is constantly running through my head right now!

What place inspires you and why?
I love downtown streets. I love light, and you can find so much beautiful light walking around the streets of Toronto.

Photography by Ardean

416.333.2850, photographybyardean.com
facebook.com/PhotographyByArdean, Twitter: @photosbyardean

Loving. Fun. Real.
Ardean loves light, people, fun and love. Her mission is to capture it all with her photography. She is inspired by documentary photography and loves using it in her wedding photography. On a portrait shoot, she incorporates her "creative lifestyle" approach, to capture the realness of expression. Ardean believes the connection made during the session is the most important part. She'd love to connect with you!

Photos by Photography by Ardean

Publisher Production Solutions

416.804.8930, publisher-ps.com
facebook.com/publisherproductionsolutions, Twitter: @publisher_ps

Classic. Creative. Stylish.
Publisher Production Solutions is an extension of a family-run printing business
that primarily prints books. A newly launched print consultant providing
advice for authors who are looking to self-publish their own books.

Q&A

What do you like best about owning a business?

Flexibility of hours for work/life balance. I'm a single parent, and I want to be able to be there for my child, but I still love working.

Who is your role model or mentor?

My parents and grandparents. In both generations, they started their own businesses and made them successful. I hope that I will have as much success as they have had.

What place inspires you and why?

I'm a visual person. I find inspiration in everything that I see. From watching TV and movies to reading magazines, different blogs or articles.

Doris Chung

Quench Trip Design

416.366.2777, quenchtravel.com, facebook.com/QuenchTripDesign, Twitter: @QuenchTravel

Savvy. Inspiring. Experiential.
Quench Trip Design handcrafts unique, customized journeys in Europe, Africa, Asia, India and the Americas. Each trip is built from scratch based on the expertise that comes from real-life experience and deep on-the-ground knowledge. Every restaurant, hotel, guide and hidden gem that travellers are sent to have made it into Quench's little black book for good reason, resulting in authentic and memorable travel experiences.

Portrait by Jessica Lin Photography

Jennifer Deacon and
Mercedeh Sanati

Q&A

What are your most popular
products or services?
Customized family getaways, honeymoons,
trips to celebrate milestone occasions and
vacations that allow people to immerse
themselves in the local culture.

What do you like best about
owning a business?
We carefully choose who we collaborate with
in each country so that we can genuinely say
that our own travel experiences and local
contacts enhance every trip that we plan.

What do you CRAVE?
The feeling we get from taking timid travellers
and turning them into fearless road warriors.
Also, the fried zucchini flowers and pici
porcini at our favourite Roman Osteria.

Chantel and Charmaine Richards

Q&A

What tip would you give women who are starting a business?
Always stay true to your passion, and never underestimate the power of hard work.

What do you like best about owning a business?
Having the satisfaction of seeing your dreams come to life and the sense of accomplishment at the end of each night.

Who is your role model or mentor?
Our role model is our parents. As entrepreneurs themselves, they have always encouraged us to depend on one another and to one day own our own company.

R&R Wedding and Event Designs

By appointment only: 1357 Weston Rd, Ste 1B, Toronto, 647.348.4442
rnrdesigns.ca, Twitter: @rnrdesigns

Creative. Resourceful. Classy.

Located in the Greater Toronto Area, R&R Wedding and Event Designs is known for creating unique, breathtaking weddings and events. As sisters, Charmaine and Chantel approach each event knowing that it may be a once-in-a-lifetime opportunity. They understand that your wedding is an emotional and financial investment; therefore, they strive to provide the finest of details without sacrificing creativity or vision.

Portrait by Maria Lalla Photography, upper-left and upper-middle photos by Manuela Stefan, upper-right photo by Phat Duo Visuals, lower-right photo by Fisher Fotographic

Sense of Independence Boutique

511 Eglinton Ave W, Toronto, 416.481.8242
senseofindependence.ca, facebook.com/senseofindependence, Twitter: @senseofind

Fresh. Addictive. Contemporary.

Sense of Independence opened in 2004 on the trendy Eglinton West strip. Sisters Naomi and Michelle knew from a young age that they loved fashion and couldn't wait to make their mark on the fashion world. With their combined experience, they have created a shopping environment that has drawn customers from around the globe to get the latest and greatest in stylish clothing and accessories.

Naomi Shamash-Zeligman
and Michelle Shamash

Q&A

What are your most popular products or services?
Our vast selection of tops. Our tops are easy to wear, can go effortlessly from day to night and have a fun twist to them, whether printed, embellished or embroidered.

What tip would you give women who are starting a business?
Don't burn yourself out and try to do everything yourself. Sometimes it's more effective to delegate tasks and focus on the more important things.

What motivates you on a daily basis?
Competition motivates us to make a lasting mark in this industry and continuously stay on top of our game.

Jacqueline Sava

Q&A

What are your most popular products or services?
Lacey, our newest Soak fragrance, is a favourite. Our foot cream and tattoos for knitters are popular as well.

What tip would you give women who are starting a business?
Planning is critical to growth. Find a mentor. Find a niche. Solve a problem. Have purpose and soul. Be inspiring. Be friendly. Be passionate. Be patient. Enjoy.

What do you like best about owning a business?
I love breaking new ground, bringing ideas to life, changing the perception of a product or industry. We revolutionized hand-washing, creating a delicate detergent people love and brag about using.

Soak Wash Inc.

By appointment only: 2465 Cawthra Rd, Ste 124, Mississauga, 905.270.SOAK (7625)
soakwash.com, facebook.com/soakwash, Twitter: @jacqueline_soak

Modern. Clean. Creative.

Soak Wash Inc. is the creative company behind the leading laundry wash for delicates. Designed for quick, clean laundry with eco-friendly ingredients, this no-rinse dream-come-true is perfect for your laciest lingerie, softest sweaters, swimwear, crafts, even baby clothes. Available in fine lingerie boutiques, yarn shops and upscale boutiques. Soak is modern care for the laundry you love. Ask for it by name.

Photos by Jessica Lin Photography

Q&A

What tip would you give women
who are starting a business?
Words of wisdom given to me from my
mentor were "asking for help is a sign
of strength, not weakness." We can't do
everything on our own; ask for help.

What do you like best about
owning a business?
I've created work for myself that is
a combination of everything I am
passionate about: business, health,
people, creating an unparalleled
customer experience, creativity, learning,
teaching and personal growth.

What motivates you on a daily basis?
My desire for knowledge and my
drive to be the best me I can be.

Jennifer Best

Photos by Lemon Fresh Designs Photography

Steeped and Infused

1258 Queen St E, Toronto, 647.348.1669
steepedandinfused.com, facebook.com/steepedinfused, Twitter: @steepedinfused

Peaceful. Healthy. Sensual.
Steeped and Infused offers more than 85 premium-quality loose-leaf tea blends, an array of unique accessories and fabulous gift items. Born out of Jennifer's personal health challenges, particularly the effects of fibromyalgia, and the benefits she received from tea, Jennifer has created a business that is an extension of who she is and what she believes in: community, education, passion, health and fun!

STLTO WINE

stltowine.com, facebook.com/STLTO, Twitter: @STLTO_WINE

Trendy. Classic. Versatile.

STLTO is a seriously stylish wine from Italy, where both fashion and wine making are world-renowned. Picked from 40-year-old vines in the lush Abruzzo region, the grapes used to create the STLTO collection deliver gorgeous colour and density. The STLTO collection is playful, seductive and versatile. From start to finish, only women are involved with this brand. Available at the LCBO (Liquor Control Board of Ontario).

 # Q&A

What tip would you give women who are starting a business?
Repeat: determination, perseverance and confidence! Take your wonderful ideas and execute them. Nothing is impossible, but you may need to approach the situation differently or find that key connection.

What is your motto or theme song?
"Do one thing every day that scares you." —Eleanor Roosevelt

What place inspires you and why?
I must say that London, England, truly inspires me. It is a dynamic, creative and wonderful city. Whenever I visit, I feel like I am on top of the world!

Sarah Liberatore

Stonefox Jewelry

1693 Avenue Rd, Toronto, 647.343.9069
shop.stonefox.ca, facebook.com/StonefoxJewelry, Twitter: @StonefoxJewelry

Natural. Expressive. Timeless.

Stonefox is a jewelry-lover's treasure trove of handmade, one-of-a-kind jewelry with semiprecious stones. Designer Andrea Tsanos's diverse collections range from dainty to chunky, short to long and layered, and the stunning selection makes it hard to leave without finding a treasure (or two!). There's even a line for little darlings: Stonefox Girl, featuring gemstone necklaces, beautiful bracelets and beading kits that make for unique gifts.

Andrea Tsanos

Q&A

What are your most popular products or services?
Our Accent Nugget statement necklaces. And our Lariat design: one long, continuous rope of gemstones that can be tied in four fabulous ways. Women love the versatility and the wow factor!

What do you like best about owning a business?
The boutique has given me the opportunity to give birth to another "baby" and to run every aspect with such creative freedom. It's never-ending hard work yet pure bliss all in one!

Who is your role model or mentor?
Fellow jewelry designer Tricia McMaster of Green Bijou and Katie Dupuis at Chatelaine/Rogers with her savvy guidance and generous spirit.

Clare Kumar

Q&A

What tip would you give women who are starting a business?
Figure out what you're really good at and what makes you feel blissful. Over time, hire help for the aspects you're not as good at or don't enjoy doing.

What motivates you on a daily basis?
What I do enables others to spend more time doing what they love, giving their gifts to the world. That's both motivating and rewarding.

How do you relax?
Singing is my favourite thing to do! I always feel better while I'm singing and for a good while after. I also like to whack a tennis ball.

Streamlife
an organizing company

647.444.3535, streamlife.ca
facebook.com/streamlife, Twitter: @streamlife, linkedin.com/in/clarekumar

Inspiring. Resourceful. Perceptive.

Streamlife offers professional organizing services to deliver greater productivity and peace of mind, both at home and at work. With a wealth of knowledge and resourcefulness, and a relentless focus on their clients' definitions of success, Chief Organizer Clare Kumar and her team of organizers and productivity consultants help people live and work the way they've always imagined.

Paola Girotti

Q&A

What are your most popular products or services?
By far, our Brazilian and eyebrow sugaring are our most popular services. We offer several hair removal combination packages as well.

What tip would you give women who are starting a business?
Make sure that you are financially stable, very clear on your vision for your business and hire a business coach.

What motivates you on a daily basis?
My two children and inspiring them. I am also motivated to create something to change other people's lives for the better.

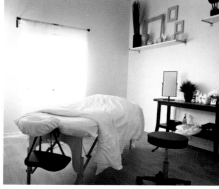

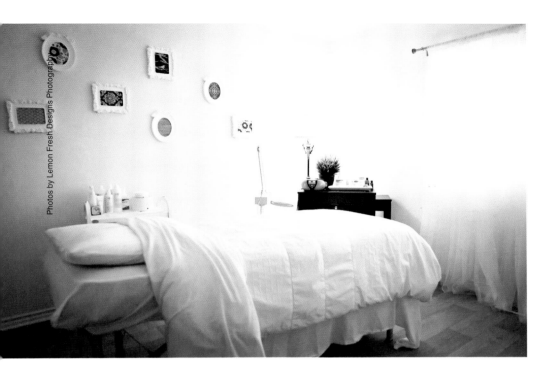

Photos by Lemon Fresh Designs Photography

SUGARMOON

1509 Danforth Ave, Toronto, 416.693.0355
2 College St, Ste 202, Toronto, 416.215.7216
sugarmoonsalon.com, facebook.com/SUGARMOONSALON
Twitter: @SUGARMOONSALON

Professional. Friendly. Unique.
SUGARMOON is Toronto's sweet alternative to waxing! Their high-end
boutiques offer hair removal with sugar paste, a 100% natural formula.
SUGARMOON's reputation for pairing their hygenic method with superior
services has attracted many high-profile celebrities. SUGARMOON has also
launched their own signature line of skincare products. SUGARMOON has
two locations in Toronto: East York and downtown at Yonge and College.

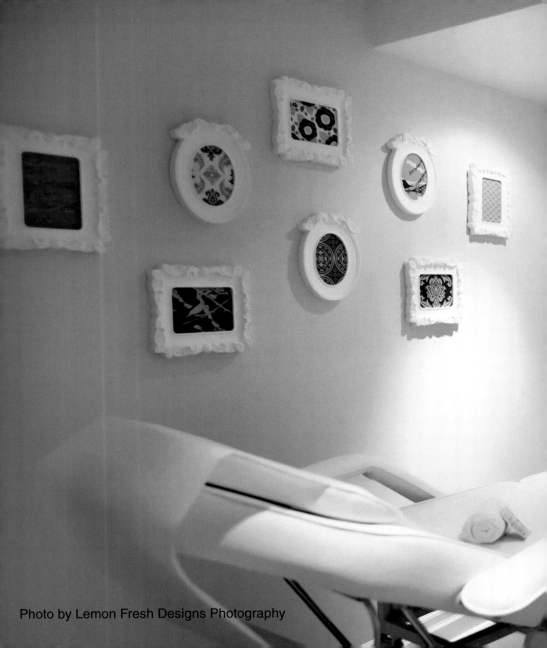
Photo by Lemon Fresh Designs Photography

" *I like seeing my vision come into action.* **"**

Paola Girotti of SUGARMOON

THEIT

647.299.1447, lovetheit.com, facebook.com/loveTHEIT, Twitter: @theitbags

Functional. Practical. Versatile.

THEIT creates camera bags for photographers who value both style and substance. With designs that aim to capture classic modernity with a sense of playfulness, this philosophy exemplifies the essence of the THEIT customer: someone who is independent, inspired and full of life, who cannot help but capture the beauty in her world through the lens.

Nicole Fajardo

Q&A

What are your most popular products or services?
Our camera bags, most especially our the Bossi Bag. It is classy but with an edge. Functional and yet versatile. It is so popular, it's hard to keep in stock!

What do you like best about owning a business?
I like that I work for myself. I like that I am challenged daily. I love that my work is flexible and allows me to spend more time with my family.

What do you CRAVE?
Success, loving family, good friends, good health, a life of travel and music. I crave the inspired life.

Dr. Jennifer Wise and Dr. Kristin Heins

Q&A

What tip would you give women
who are starting a business?
It is much easier to be successful at
something you are passionate about,
so follow your heart and your dreams.

What do you like best about
owning a business?
The sense of accomplishment that comes
from watching our hard work materialize.
Not having a boss is pretty nice, too!

What motivates you on a daily basis?
The drive to be our best selves and
provide amazing care to our patients.
People telling us that they are feeling
great is the ultimate inspiration.

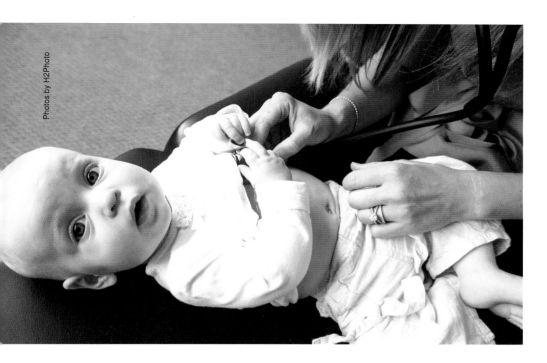

Thrive Natural Family Health

By appointment only: 110 Eglinton Ave E, Ste 502, Toronto, 647.352.7911
thrivehealth.ca, Twitter: @thrivenfamilyh

Empowering. Holistic. Supportive.
Thrive Natural Family Health is a midtown multidisciplinary clinic including
naturopathic, chiropractic and registered massage therapy services. They care for
individuals of all ages and stages, and have a unique focus in young family care and
specific training in pregnancy and pediatrics. It is their priority to help every patient
thrive and achieve greater health in a setting that is both chic and family-friendly.

Toronto's Careerist

torontoscareerist.com, Twitter: @TOsCareerist

Ambitious. Creative. Intimate.

A Toronto-based company providing photography and event planning services. In a diverse, multicultural city filled with a wide range of talent, Toronto's Careerist strives to discover and brand unique individuals who are up and coming and pursuing their dreams, capturing their story and the essence of their craft through their lens.

Lower-left photos and portrait by Photography by Ardean, upper-right photos by Alicia D. Johnson

MADE.WITH.LOVE.

ANA BOGDANOVIC

Jewelry as an art form has the power to create a mood provoke an opinion and produce a reaction. Each piece is uniquely handmade and designed

Alicia D. Johnson

Q&A

What do you like best about owning a business?
Thinking outside the box with different projects, trying out new techniques. Being really creative with my suggestions to clients when planning a photo shoot or intimate, exclusive dinner events.

Who is your role model or mentor?
I have a list of well-known photographers I look to as role models. When it comes to event/wedding planners, Toronto's own Jade Lee is a truly inspiring mentor.

What motivates you on a daily basis?
My daughters. They each have a creatively talented mind. Every day I draw inspiration from the little things they say and do.

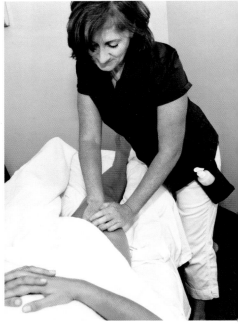
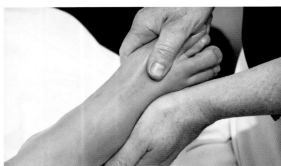

Total Body Chiropractic Therapy Clinic

601 Kingston Rd, Ste 107, Toronto, 416.699.9990
totalbodychiro.com, Twitter @totalbodychiro

Professional. Hands-on. Compassionate.

Dr. Patricia McCord has carefully selected her team of practitioners, creating a positive and uplifting atmosphere conducive to healing. The team consists of seven unique women, all whom share the same mantra: to optimize health and well-being through individualized care programs and in a positive environment. All services are natural, hands-on and complementary to one another, ranging from chiropractic, naturopathic, Chinese medicine and acupuncture to therapeutic massage and hypnotherapy.

Patricia McCord and Her Team

Q&A

What is the key to customer loyalty?
Our insistence on individualized patient-focused care. Through therapy and education, patients have the ability to take charge of their own health.

What are your signature treatments or services?
We offer a new and highly effective treatment for frozen shoulder called the OTZ Technique, dramatically increasing range of motion and restoring function while decreasing pain. We also emphasize a "Total Body" approach, including diet and nutrition, massage and full-body correction.

What motivates and inspires you?
Observing the positive changes that our patients achieve in their lives—that is the driving force that inspires each and every member of the team. We elevate the quality of life of each person we see by reducing pain, increasing function and mobility and improving lifestyle choices.

"I just love being a chiropractor and I appreciate the opportunity to mentor and collaborate with other professionals. We enjoy working together for the betterment of our patients."

Patricia McCord of Total Body Chiropractic Therapy Clinic

Q&A

What are your most popular products or services?
Facilitation of powerful group conversations and learning experiences. Action research: an approach that enables organizations to see themselves differently and to determine their own solutions. Integral coaching for personal change.

What tip would you give women who are starting a business?
Start by committing to the kind of life you want to live, then build your business to respond to that.

What do you like best about owning a business?
Blending working and living with an adaptive schedule. "Being me" as my business.

What motivates you on a daily basis?
Seeing the exhilarating impact that I can have on shifting perspectives from limited to expanded, moving reluctance toward conviction, steering darkness toward light, isolation toward connection and criticism toward appreciation.

What is your motto or theme song?
"Change is disturbing when it's done to us, exhilarating when it's done by us." —Rosabeth Moss Kantner

Tracey Peever

Tracey Peever
Human Systems Process Consultant

416.939.5012, traceypeever.com, Twitter: @tflo

Evolutionary. Progressive. Human-centered.
Tracey is a unique consultant for complex modern times. She helps organizations, groups and individuals to connect to the heart of what matters and to enact purposeful change, using methods that are participative, not prescriptive. She is a creative experience designer, facilitator, and coach who specializes in helping people examine the relationship between *how* they work (process) and the quality of *what* they do.

Photos by IrinaPhotography

Q & A

What tip would you give women
who are starting a business?
Only pursue an idea you are passionate
about. Being a business owner requires an
enormous commitment, so you want to be
involved with something you really love.

What do you like best about
owning a business?
The freedom to follow my passion
and focus on what interests me.
I love the jewelry, but I'm also
fascinated by the styles, makers
and social history of the times.

What motivates you on a daily basis?
The quest for outstanding pieces
of jewelry and little-known facts
about jewelry makers.

Barbara A. Schwartz

trufaux
JEWELS

Vintage Costume Jewelry
& Accessories

www.trufauxjewels.com

TruFaux Jewels

trufauxjewels.com, 416.690.7766, facebook.com/trufauxjewels

Vintage. Elegant. Stylish.
TruFaux Jewels presents the best in vintage costume jewelry from 1920 through
1960 by Hattie Carnegie, Elsa Schiaparelli and other notable American and
European makers who took jewelry design into the realm of art. Each piece has
a look and a story that is guaranteed to reach out and touch not just collectors
but every woman who wants to create her own style and mode of expression.

UrbanMommies Media

604.418.4800, urbanmommies.com, Twitter: @urbanmommies

Engaging. Aware. Connected.
Comprising the successful successful online lifestyle magazines UrbanMommies.
com and UrbanDaddies.com, UrbanMommies Media has evolved into a trusted brand
for thousands of chic parents across Canada. Driven by the desire to ensure that
parents don't lose their identities once they've had kids, the publications feature family
travel, funky family recipes, parenting tips, and tech and fashion for savvy parents.

Lower-left photo and upper-middle photo by Bopomo Pictures

Jill Amery

Q&A

What are your most popular products or services?
We reach families via the magazines as well as Pinterest, Facebook, RSS, newsletters, Twitter and through YouTube on the new UrbanMommies TV. Parents can pick their favourite way to engage.

What tip would you give women who are starting a business?
Outsource tasks that you're not interested in doing and consult with other entrepreneurs about your business plan. Revisit your plan often.

Who is your role model or mentor?
Walt Disney. He said, "We are not trying to entertain the critics. I'll take my chances with the public."

Vital Steps Inc

1701A Avenue Rd, North York, 416.785.8828
vitalsteps.com, Twitter: @vital_steps

Healthy. Wholistic. Attentive.
Vital Steps is a personalized fitness and lifestyle studio located in Toronto, Canada.
Staffed and networked with medical exercise specialists, group class instructors,
certified personal training professionals, including medical doctors, physiotherapists,
chiropractors, and massage therapists who, combined, offer decades of experience,
providing clients with customized exercise programs with an emphasis on integrating
exercise with rehabilitation and weight and nutrition management programs.

 **Q&A**

What is the key to customer loyalty?
It begins with our team of health, medical
and lifestyle professionals, program pricing,
convenient and accessible location and
the attitudinal loyalty of our clients.

What are your signature services?
Customized personal training and rehabilitation
programs including medically based fitness
programs, specialty classes, Zoomer programs
and student/teen athletic programs.

What tip would you give women
who are starting a business?
Do the research, write a business plan,
be professional from the get-go, get
clients first, start your business while still
employed and, lastly, don't do it alone.

Jo-Ann James

" I enjoy the freedom to make decisions and live by them. "

Jo-Ann James of Vital Steps Inc

Photo by Jessica Lin Photography

Natalie Jamison

 Q&A

What are your most popular
products or services?
Financial snapshots: a summary
graph and table that forecasts your
future financial health. A picture is
worth a thousand words, so these
"snapshots" are priceless.

What tip would you give women
who are starting a business?
Surround yourself with great
advisors for legal, tax and investment
expertise. Inject your personality
into the business. Find a mentor.

What do you like best about
owning a business?
Flexibility in my schedule. Ability to
create my own future. No glass ceiling.

Women & Wealth®
RBC Dominion Securities

By appointment only: 435 North Service Rd W, Ste 301, Oakville
905.469.7074, 800.567.5615, www.jamison.ca

Savvy. Unique. Caring.
Women & Wealth is a boutique-style wealth management service, offered
exclusively through RBC Dominion Securities. It provides a highly personalized
environment for investing—a place where dreams, goals and visions get
taken care of. With a woman's perspective on financial planning, Natalie helps
entrepreneurs and families create, protect and pass wealth to the next generation.

Photos by H2Photo

AWESOME CLIENT MEETING IN PROGRESS

WSUP Toronto

Diana: 416.725.7735, Gudrun: 416.834.5801
wsuptoronto.ca, Twitter: @wsuptoronto

Empowering. Zen. Athletic.
WSUP Toronto is a Stand Up Paddleboard company in the Toronto Beaches that offers board
rentals, sales, private and group lessons, corporate team-building events, Liquid Yoga, Board
Bootcamp and excursions. They have 14 boards and are ready to go in summer 2012!

Diana Turnbull and Gudrun Hardes

Q&A

What are your most popular products or services?
Board rentals, Board Bootcamp and Liquid Yoga.

What tip would you give women who are starting a business?
Do your homework, do your research, know your market and most of all do something you have a passion for.

What place inspires you and why?
Sayulita a small Surf town north of Puerto Vallarta. No big box hotels just small mexican style villas and lots of lovely organic restaurants. Also the best passionfruit margaritas!

X-Design INC.

1135 Dundas St, Ste 200, Toronto, 416.462.3084 x233
xdesigninc.com

Intelligent. Intuitive. Unpretentious.
X-Design is a full-scope interior design and project management firm. They work with clients to create and build beautiful spaces. The most important part of any environment is the people who inhabit the space. Their designs comfort, support, motivate and embrace those who dwell within. Their expertise encompasses custom homes and developments, dynamic work environments and high-impact retail spaces.

Susan Quinn and Cathy Knott

Q&A

What tip would you give women
who are starting a business?
Do something you enjoy and can get
satisfaction from by contributing to make a
difference. With passion comes success.

What do you like best about
owning a business?
Being in control of our own success.

Who is your role model or mentor?
Our children are our role models: always
honest and always interested in learning more.

What motivates you on a daily basis?
We are motivated when we get to talk to a
happy client. The connection between us
and our clients is essential and satisfying.

Q&A

What are your most popular products or services?
At the moment, the most popular packages are those that include styling and personal shopping as well as branding for small businesses.

What tip would you give women who are starting a business?
Launch your business with a strong brand that truly represents you and what you intend to accomplish. Be strategic and flexible over time with your personal and professional image.

What do you like best about owning a business?
I love the freedom to constantly create new projects and services.

Zayna Mosam,
BA (Hons), AICI CIP

Zayna Mosam Image Consulting
Inspire your future...

■ ■ ■ ■ ■

Personal & Corporate Programs

branding strategy

style & wardrobe analysis

personal shopping excursions

public image development

etiquette & protocol coaching

interpersonal communications

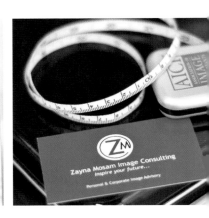

Zayna Mosam
Image Consulting

By appointment only: 285 Manitoba Dr, Studio 5, Toronto, 416.907.8156
zmimage.com, Twitter: @ZaynaMosam

Contemporary. Creative. Sophisticated.
Zayna Mosam Image Consulting was launched in 2003 and provides
customized programs for men and women, private groups and corporations.
Services include image and lifestyle management, communications
coaching, etiquette and protocol coaching, personal shopping, personal
branding, styling and public image development. Zayna is a Certified
Image Professional (CIP), speaker, writer and frequent media guest who
has appeared on CTV, Citytv, MuchMusic, Bravo, BNN and more.

$\mathcal{I}nde\chi$ by Category

by Category (continued)

by Category (continued)

ꟿ𝓷𝓭𝓮𝔁 by Neighbourhood

by Neighbourhood (continued)

by Neighbourhood (continued)

Contributors

We believe in acknowledging, celebrating and passionately supporting locally owned businesses and entrepreneurs. We are extremely grateful to all contributors for this publication.

Melody Biringer

CRAVE Founder

thecravecompany.com startupjunkie.com

Innovative. Feminine. Connective.
Melody Biringer, self-avowed "start-up junkie," has built companies that range from Biringer Farm, a family-run specialty-food business, to home furnishings to a fitness studio.

Her current entrepreneurial love-child is The CRAVE Company: designed to creatively connect entrepreneurs who approach business in a fresh new way with the consumers they desire, as well as with each other. CRAVE is a resource for women entrepreneurs to promote their business and support like-minded women, and CRAVEguides are your go-to source for anything you could ever wish to find in your city—exclusively from women. Melody has taken CRAVE from Seattle to more than 30 cities worldwide, including New York City, Boston, Los Angeles, Chicago, Amsterdam and Toronto. Melody is a loyal community supporter, versed traveler and strong advocate for women-owned businesses.

Andrea Rocca

CRAVE Toronto Partner

Twitter: @Andrea_Rocca

Creative. Connected. Innovative.
Raised in a family of entrepreneurs, it was never a surprise that Andrea would eventually catch the entrepreneurial bug herself. After receiving her BBA with an honour in marketing, Andrea gained experience working in the marketing departments of two global companies before joining the CRAVE team.

As an early adopter of social media, Andrea has loved being able to put her digital talents to use, promoting the fantastic and diverse group of women that are CRAVE Toronto. Helping grow this community of talented and motivated entreprenesses has been a wonderful opportunity.

Andrea's personal (and hopefully, one day, professional) passions include all things related to food and drink, fashion and design.

Brooke Milne

CRAVE Toronto Partner

647.927.4790, becauseyousaidso.net
Twitter: @MissMilne, @BecauseUSaidSo
missentreprenette.tumblr.com

Organized. Bubbly. Independent.
Brooke is a self-proclaimed workaholic and loves to stay busy with a variety of opportunities. Having grown up in the digital generation, she has been bitten by the social media bug and loves to explore all it has to offer.

A creative soul at heart, Brooke is constantly craving change. Shortly after launching Because You Said So... Promotions and Events with her mom, she began working for CRAVE and DivaGirl Fitness. These positions have allowed her to flourish in the entrepreneurial world, by combining her love of marketing and events with her knowledge of social media.

Brooke is passionate about entrepreneurship among women and is committed to helping women follow their dreams and create something magical. She accomplishes this through her work with CRAVE and DivaGirl Preneur and their amazing communities.

When Brooke is not busy working, she is teaching young children to ski at Caledon Ski Club.

Contributors

Alison Turner, *Graphic Designer*

alisonjturner.com, linkedin.com/in/alisont

Alison is a passionate designer and critical thinker from Seattle. She supports human rights and the local food movement. She enjoys researching interesting things, volunteering, being outside, dancing, cooking and running.

Amanda Buzard, *Lead Designer*

amandabuzard.com

Amanda is a Seattle native inspired by clean patterns and vintage design. She chases many creative and active pursuits in her spare time, including photography, baking, attempting DIY projects and exploring the beautiful Pacific Northwest.

Carrie Wicks, *Copy Editor*

linkedin.com/in/carriewicks

Carrie has been proofreading professionally for 14-plus years in mostly creative fields. When she's not proofreading/copyediting, she's reading, singing jazz, walking in the woods or gardening.

Christine Reid Photography, *Photographer*

christinereidphotoblog.com, Twitter: @creidphoto

As a natural light portrait photographer, I adore mixing nature and simplicity during a session to create naturally candid moments. I also love bacon way more than I should.

IrinaPhotography, *Photographer*

irinaphotography.ca

Irina Fortey is a contemporary lifestyle portrait photographer whose work is best described as emotional and creative. Her unique and personalized approach demonstrates her high dedication to capturing authentic images for her clients. She has been published in numerous publications and has garnered several awards for her work.

Jessica Lin Photography, *Photographer*

416.806.1585, jessicalin.ca, Twitter: @jessicalinphoto

Jessica Lin is a photographer who loves capturing the beauty of real moments, pretty things and fantastic locations. She lives for the fulfillment of a shot well taken.

Lemon Fresh Designs Photography, *Photographer*

lemonfreshdesigns.com, 416.918.6817

Lemon Fresh Designs Photography specializes in modern, stylish wedding and lifestyle photography. Mary's creative use of natural light creates stylish and timeless imagery for her clients in Toronto or Muskoka.

Maria Lalla, *Photographer*

marialalla.com, lallastudios.com, marialalla.tumblr.com
Twitter: @maria_lalla, facebook.com/MMariaLalla

Maria Lalla specializes in photography for commercial, publicity, portfolio, wedding or personal needs. Providing a wealth of experience to clients from large corporations to small-business owners.

Photography by Ardean, *Photographer*

photographybyardean.com, 416.333.2850

Ardean specializes in portraiture and wedding photography, with a love for photojournalistic-style shooting. She enjoys taking photos of people, beautiful light and capturing the world around her.

Thank you to our additional contributors: CRAVE Toronto interns Colleen Imrie and Victoria (Vikki) Yee, and photographer Maryam Toson.

Get the savings you crave with the following participating businesses—one time only!

- [ ] Alma Natural Quick Spa
  15% discount

- [ ] Amalsroom.com
  $25 discount on an order of $100 or more

- [ ] bebo mia inc.
  $100 off initial services booked

- [ ] Because You Said So...
  10% discount

- [ ] Blossom Lounge
  20% discount (regular-priced items only)

- [ ] body politic
  20% discount (regular-priced items only)

- [ ] Cafe Novo
  free cookie with any drink purchase

- [ ] Calligraphy by Diane
  10% discount (first-time clients only)

- [ ] Coco & Lily Flowers Ltd
  30% discount

- [ ] distill gallery
  15% off (full-price items only)

- [ ] eLUXE
  15% discount (valid through 2013)

- [ ] Escapeto Travel Lifestyle
  10% discount

- [ ] Evolving Being
  $20 off a personal session

- [ ] The Feather Factory
  15% discount

- [ ] Fuzz Wax Bar
  25% discount

- [ ] Georgie Porgie Cakes & Gifts
  20% discount

- [ ] H2Photo
  $25 print credit with any portrait session

- [ ] I Heart Accessories
  20% discount

- [ ] ideal samples Inc.
  complimentary 30-minute idea consultation

- [ ] in2art Gallery
  10% discount

- [ ] IrinaPhotography
  10% discount

- [ ] Jessica Lin Photography
  10% discount

- [ ] Kathleen's Closet
  $50 towards a wardrobe consultation

- [ ] Kathryn L. Smithen, Barrister, Solicitor & Notary Public
  free one-hour consultation

- [ ] Lilliput Hats
  20% discount

- [ ] Luxe Moments Lifestyle
  10% discount

- [ ] MANGIA & BEVI resto-bar
  15% off entire purchase (does not include alcohol)

- [ ] **Maria Lalla Photography**
  free engagement photo shoot with booking of wedding

- [ ] **The Mercantile**
  15% discount

- [ ] **Mildred & Doris Gift Studio**
  20% discount

- [ ] **momcafé Network Inc.**
  50% off virtual membership

- [ ] **Morris Feng Shui**
  10% discount

- [ ] **MSC Fitness**
  10% off membership (1–6 months)

- [ ] **Nancy Falconi Inc**
  free custom portrait consultation

- [ ] **nicenook**
  25% discount

- [ ] **Nour-ish**
  20% discount

- [ ] **Ohhh Canada**
  free mini Blossom Organics lube

- [ ] **Orangefish**
  25% off first purchase

- [ ] **Publisher Production Solutions**
  free print consultation + free ISBN registrations and barcode creation (value $150)

- [ ] **R&R Wedding and Event Designs**
  15% discount

- [ ] **Sense of Independence Boutique**
  10% discount

- [ ] **Soak Wash Inc.**
  15% discount

- [ ] **Steeped and Infused**
  20% discount on loose leaf teas

- [ ] **Stonefox Jewelry**
  15% discount (in store only)

- [ ] **Streamlife, an organizing company**
  10% discount

- [ ] **SUGARMOON**
  25% off a sugaring hair removal service

- [ ] **THEIT**
  15% off a THEIT bag

- [ ] **Thrive Natural Family Health**
  $30 off initial chiropractic or naturopathic visit

- [ ] **Tracey Peever, Human Systems Process Consultant**
  20% off an individual coaching session

- [ ] **Urban Mode**
  15% discount

- [ ] **Vital Steps**
  free body analysis with purchase of a class or a personal training package

- [ ] **Women & Wealth® RBC Dominion Securities**
  complimentary second opinion (a confidential, objective review of your investment portfolio)

- [ ] **WSUP Toronto**
  10% discount

Use code CRAVE for online discount when applicable.

Details of discounts may vary from business to business, so please call first.
The CRAVE company shall not be held responsible for variations on discounts at individual businesses. This page may not be photocopied or otherwise duplicated.